This Is God Speaking

A Commentary on the Book of Hebrews

GLENN VELLEKAMP

authorHOUSE®

AuthorHouse™
1663 Liberty Drive
Bloomington, IN 47403
www.authorhouse.com
Phone: 1 (800) 839-8640

Published by AuthorHouse   11/23/2016

ISBN: 978-1-5246-5206-7 (sc)
ISBN: 978-1-5246-5205-0 (e)

Contents

Introduction

We're not sure why it's called "Hebrews" and we're not sure who wrote it. But from reading the Bible for over forty years, to me it is one of the deepest letters ever written. It will be important to stick to the facts if we're going to make a useful and revealing commentary and in referring to what is factual, I mean referring to the Bible. I will be using the Bible to establish facts. So although atheists, agnostics and devotees of other religions might read this, it's not really to them. It's for the Christian. I believe this letter called "Hebrews" is a startling description of who Jesus is and who we are because of him. I think that there are several authors that may have contributed to this compilation, one of them saying that most people reading it won't get it (Heb 5:11ff). We certainly have our work cut out for us. It contains many references to the TaNaKh (the Old Testament books) and may be why someone thought it was addressed to Hebrews or Jews and should be called Hebrews. Some call it "Messianics" meaning followers of the Messiah from Judaism. I think the epistle is to all Christians from all back rounds and although I value the words of Christ above all others, I think we should all use the whole Bible.

Using the Bible as the text for facts, letting the Bible define the concepts in this letter, not denominational beliefs or traditional practices, I will try to differentiate what is "fact" and what is my own opinion or conclusion. So feel free to challenge any of my deductions, opinions and conclusions but when biblical facts are cited just know there is no challenge, well, except in our own minds because of what we have been spoon fed previously. Some have started denominations and other "churches" based on "God spoke to me directly". I am not one of those. The only time I think that God speaks to me is when I am reading the red words, and they are available to everyone. I don't have a direct line to God for special revelation. I am your fellow servant; no more, no less.

It would be helpful to have read other books I have written but not necessarily required. I will try to make this book stand on its own. However, I will refer to the other books and in doing so I will use abbreviations. (*A View Worth Teaching*, under the pen name Tim Tyler, will be AV,

The Samaritan Woman You Never Knew is TSW, *They Heard What They Thought He Meant* is TH, and *Who Is Jesus* is WIJ). This is not to promote buying my other books but they may provide explanation on how we connect biblical dots.

I believe any believer, any follower of Christ, can receive any of the ideas or "revelations" that we are discussing here just by reading the Bible. I don't think anything we discuss here is a private or a sole revelation revealed only to me. I just haven't heard anyone else express things this way and therefore feel the need to write this commentary. In all my writings and talks I have had one goal, namely to excite the reader or listener to read the Bible and see if these things are so. I desire to encourage and motivate you to read and dig in your Bible until the "facts" convince you. In doing so I think God will be speaking to you through the Bible. I won't be doing your exercise for you, just merely driving you to the gym so that you can do the work.

I would think that if you are a preacher or teacher, there would be enough covered here to give you sermons for at least a year. Whether you agree or disagree, you could preach with these thoughts and expound on them or disagree and expound on that. The end result is that real believers will read their Bibles and come to their own conclusions. You may quote me and use my name or quote me and not use any reference to me. Truth is truth and I don't own it.

So as we get started please have your Bible and concordance on hand and your mind focused on the facts. The text will be dependent on you looking up Bible verses and chapter and verse may not always be cited.

Please note that the chapters in this book will be following the chapters in the epistle called "Hebrews".

1

God

It is interesting that in all the other epistles (letters), the authors identify themselves first, for example, "James, to…..", "Paul, to ……", "Peter, to…..", John calls himself "the elder, to…" and "Jude, to….". In most translations, "Hebrews" starts with "God…..spoke". I think that one of the writers of "Hebrews" is Jesus himself. That's just my opinion. I think Jesus wrote this first part about who he is, because no one else really could. The fact is that the writer is saying that God used to speak through the prophets but NOW in these last days has spoken through his Son. That means that before Christ, God spoke through his servants the prophets but when he revealed himself in the Son, in Christ, he no longer spoke through prophets but through the body he created for himself. "God was in Christ reconciling the world unto himself" (2 Cor 5:19). There are many translations; we will be using the original Greek to English by Jay P. Green, Sr. for our default reference. I think that what is usually printed in red words, the words of Christ in red, <u>are</u> God's words and the words of the prophets <u>were</u> God's words, but the rest are men's words through their own minds as they were inspired by the Holy Spirit to write about what the prophets and Jesus had said. Moses was a prophet and wrote about God's character. In Exodus 34:6-7 Moses writes what God said about himself and I believe these words are timeless, "…..Merciful, gracious and slow to anger, great in goodness and truth, keeping mercy……forgiving (and yet just)". What if God is more merciful than we think? Or could even imagine? I also believe that David was a prophet and that some of the Psalms are God speaking through David. Having said that, I believe the whole Bible to be true, an accurate account of what people said. I believe that Job's friends really said what is recorded. I believe that what Satan said to Jesus is also accurate. But it would be foolish to say that Satan's words are the word of God. So I believe that only Jesus' words <u>are</u> the word of God and only the words of the prophets <u>were</u> the word of God. Also any time the word "scripture" is used in the "new testament" books, it is always a reference to the books of the "old testament". Please make a study of this. There are no new testament "scriptures" (writings); there are "writings" but none of the new testament writers referred to their letters or others' letters as "scripture". It seems strange to say that but remember as the apostles wrote in the new testament they referred to that which was already written (Greek word "graphe" 1124 in Strong's, translated scripture) and the only thing that was written was the old testament (or the TaNaKh). There is one place where Peter talks about Paul's writings as being hard to understand, which meant that he must have heard of or seen some of Paul's writings. This would be building a doctrine on one verse, out of its context and it is mistranslated as well. The correct translation is "as also the remaining (3062) scriptures " not "as the other scriptures"(2 Pet 3:16). So it's only talking about the remaining scriptures, the TaNaKh, or what we call the Old Testament, not saying that Paul's writings are scripture like the "other scriptures". This is a sore point with those who want to say that every word in the Bible is the word of God and is scripture, because like other faulty doctrinal beliefs, it relies totally on one verse. It's not sacrilegious to say that Paul didn't know sometimes whether it was God speaking through him or just him speaking; he said that himself (1 Cor 7). And in one place he said it wasn't the Lord (1 Cor 7:12). Paul also said he only knew in part (1 Cor 13:9). Jesus did not know only in part. His words are Spirit and Life and though heaven and earth will pass away Jesus' words will never pass away. They are not bound to time and space. The apostles wrote what they understood in part. God did not magically move their fingers to write the everlasting word of God. They wrote through their own understanding, what they thought he meant (read TH). (see abbreviations in the introduction) When Jesus revealed his glory to the three apostles in

Matthew 17, the message was clear, "This is my Son, hear him"! Moses and Elijah were there at first but then only Jesus was there. The law, represented by Moses, and the prophets, represented by Elijah were God's voice and they were scripture, but Jesus said, "Search the scriptures........they speak of me" (Jn 5:39). In Luke 24:27 and 44 Jesus tells the two disciples that everything from Moses and all the prophets is about himself.

God appointed his Son heir of all; through whom he made everything. This means that the Son in a body, in whom he spoke was the beginning of all creation in which God created everything else. There is a reference to that in Revelation 3:14; Jesus Christ refers to himself as "The beginning of the creation of God". I don't think there is anyone more qualified to tell us about the Son than himself. Let's listen as he takes us through the messianic psalms that forecast his coming. (Heb 1:2) He is the "shining splendor of his glory", as the three apostles found out in Matthew 17. He is the express "image" of his essence and upholding ALL things by the word of his power. This man, this body that God created for himself before he created anything else is the body which he used to create everything else. But this body was not God. This was a created being, not created of anything that was made (Col 1:13ff). God, the Creator, is Spirit (John 4:24) and created a body in which to express himself. The Spirit, the eternal Godhead, reproduced himself (Son) and poured himself (Spirit), not all of himself, because God is everywhere, but filled the image he made for himself with his Spirit. He knew when he made that body that it would suffer and die for his most wonderful creation, mankind, whom he would create for a love relationship. He did all this before anything else was created. I don't pretend to understand all of the workings of the spirit realm, but I know that Paul speaks of spiritual bodies and natural bodies. Also there are two kinds of natural bodies, the immortal body and the mortal body. In the beginning I believe the first body that the Creator created was a spiritual body. Then there was the immortal body in which he visited Earth. He made Adam from the earth. He visited Adam, Enoch, Abraham, Joshua, Hagar and Solomon, in a body, referred to as Melchizedek in some places, referred to as the Angel of the Lord in others. Then there was the mortal body that was birthed through Mary. The plan was in motion. He would purify us, mankind, of our sins by himself. He would redeem us. This is something he chose to do. He didn't ask for counsel or permission or even our input. He decided by his will that he would redeem us, and his grace is sufficient to do that. He sat down on the right of the majesty on high……. "Okay, so He, Jesus, sat down on the right of God? There are two"? No. There is one. Our natural tendency here is to picture in our minds what God looks like, maybe the ceiling of the Sistine Chapel, but we must understand that spirit is never physical. The Sistine Chapel is beautiful but it's not the Bible. There is one God, the Spirit. He reproduced his spirit, not physical, the Son, but it's the same spirit, the Holy Spirit and made a body in which the Spirit could work. In our "Christianese" dialogue we say things like, "God is in me and God is in you". What we mean by that is that the Spirit of God is in me and in you. And we understand that we don't mean that there are two Gods, one in me and one in you, and then there are all the others who have God in them. He is not two persons, or three. So, God can't be split up into many gods, but He is everywhere at the same time, omnipresent. God's name is Jesus, (well, in English it is but in Hebrew it's Yahwehshua or Yeshua). The Son in the body called "the Christ" came in his Father's name, Yeshua, translated "Jesus" in English, and it literally means, "God saves". There is one God. He is Spirit. His name is Jesus. He is our Father. Father, Son and Holy Spirit are three words we use to describe God's nature, but God could never be described as three of anything. He's not three spirits. He's not three persons. He's not three entities. He's not three personalities. He's not three of anything. He is not two of anything. He is one. There is a verse in 1 John 5:7 that is included in some Bibles and not included in others. It was added to the original manuscripts of John's first letter in the fourth century but was not in the original. It says that there are three that bear witness in heaven. Well, there aren't. We don't know who added this verse or why but it doesn't clear things up. God doesn't have parts either. Jesus said, "God is a spirit" (John 4:24). One. A look through Isaiah will confirm this (especially Isa 43:11). The man Jesus Christ is not the Son of God; (I hope I didn't lose you on that one, stay with me) he's a man, a body, the man Christ Jesus, the son of man, meaning that he was born of a woman. The eternal Son of God is the Spirit in the man. This may seem complicated but only because we have been taught otherwise. The simplicity of Christ is that God was in Christ (2 Cor 5:19). God is a spirit and Christ (Messiah in Hebrew) is a man. The Son of God is spirit. The son of man is man. That which is born of the spirit is spirit; that which is born of the flesh is flesh (John 3:6). In John 17 Jesus Christ, the man, prays. In this prayer Jesus describes who he is as a man speaking about the Spirit within him which is God, the Son of God. He says, speaking to Father, that he gave his apostles "Your name" and "Your words", this means that the name "Jesus" is Father's name and the words that Jesus the man spoke were God's words. This is why the words of Jesus Christ are pre-eminent in all things. This is why the red words are God's words and the rest are applications of his word. This is why the words of Jesus are timeless and the words of others in the Bible are time stamped. This is why context or the "when and where and who" of a Bible verse are vital to understanding its meaning. Jesus the Spirit in the man says to "Glorify your Son (Spirit) with the glory which I (Spirit) had with you before the existence of the world. "Jesus" is also the name of the man. Jesus the Spirit was in Jesus the man. "Wait.......What"? Okay, today there are many named Jesus, especially in Mexico, pronounced "Hay soos". It's just a name. It doesn't mean that they are all saviors. In the same way Jesus Christ isn't the Savior because that's his name but he is the Savior of the world and that's why it is his name. "You shall call his name Jesus because he shall save his people from their sins" (Matt 1:21).

We can use earthly analogies but they are very limited. Nevertheless, we will use earthly examples to try to digest spiritual concepts. So, the Amoeba that we studied in middle school might give us some idea of how to comprehend this. When the father/mother Amoeba "births" a son (or daughter), it divides. Part of the Amoeba splits off of the one celled animal and becomes the exact same reproduction of the parent. If you've seen the "son" then you've seen the father. It's kind of like that. Well, except it's not physical. The Son, the eternal son is of the Father and He is Spirit. The Son of God is Spirit, Holy Spirit. The son of man is the physical body that housed that Spirit, birthed through the body of a woman but without being descended from her. Mary's egg wasn't involved; she was a surrogate mother. God planted a whole seed (sperm and egg, forgive the crudeness) in Mary. Jesus couldn't be a descendent from Mary who was a descendant of Adam or he would be born with a sin nature which he wasn't. He knew no sin. The Roman Catholic Church tried to "fix" this by saying that Mary was conceived without a man, hence what they call the "immaculate conception". Yes, the so called "immaculate conception" was not about Jesus but Mary's birth. In my own thinking God had to reduce the body he made for himself down to a single cell, a whole cell, a fertilized cell, programmed with all the DNA of that body and plant that into Mary's uterus. When that immortal cell attached to Mary it became mortal and grew and was born of a woman and was able to die for all of our punishment. This turns out to be a big argument from those who want to say Jesus the man was just like us, sinful flesh. He came in the "likeness" of sinful flesh, not sinful flesh. He knew no sin. They believe God put a single cell in Mary but it was just the sperm cell and it penetrated Mary's egg. If God could put a single cell in Mary, why wouldn't it be a whole cell? Why is it so hard to believe that God put a whole fertilized cell in Mary as a surrogate mother and Jesus was born of a woman but not a descendent of Adam thereby making him sinless. Jesus said, "......I am from above, ... I am not from this world...."(Jn 8:23). Being equal with God he emptied himself and took the <u>form</u> of a servant, not all knowing, omniscient; not all powerful, omnipotent; and not all present, omnipresent (Phi'p 2:6-7). Although I quote references to specific verses, I would encourage the reader to read the surrounding verses for context. If you've ever seen a wind sock at a weather station or the airport, we might get an idea of spirit there. The wind (spirit) blows and travels through the sock filling it and giving it direction. While it is in the sock it is confined and limited. This is like the Spirit of God being like the wind (Jn 3:8). The wind or spirit in the sock is of the wind outside the sock but it is limited by the sock. The sock represents the man, Christ. The sock is not the wind. Christ is not the spirit, but houses the Spirit. I believe in the divinity of Christ. This is the only man from heaven. This is the only man without sin. He is the only heavenly created man but he is not the Creator. Jesus, the Spirit in the Messiah ("Christ" in Greek) is the Creator, God. You could say that God whose name is Jesus (Yeshua, Yah saves) is in Christ ("Messiah" in Hebrew), the body he made for himself. I spoke to a young lady, a mother of two, who had been raised in the Messianic movement and did all the Sabbath things and feast days and candles and dreidels and Chanukah and all that stuff but she had no idea that "Christ" was the Greek translation of Messiah. It clarifies some things. Messianic actually means Christian. I've actually had someone ask, "Is Jesus Jewish or the first Christian"? We should know what these terms mean before we use them.

In the beginning God created the heavens and the earth. In the beginning was the Word and the Word was with God and the Word was God. God is his Word. According to John 17, Hebrews 1 and 2:10 and Colossians 1, the man, Christ Jesus was the first thing that the Creator created. Everything including the world was made through him. God put his word in a body that he prepared for himself and spoke the world into existence. The word is God but the word did not "become" flesh. I know. I know what John 1:14 says in the King James and other translations. We just need to do a quick word study to discover that the number that corresponds to the original language in the Greek to English translation is not the correct number. The Greek word in the original text is spelled "e genet o". The number assigned to the word is 1096 in the Strong's concordance, which is spelled "gin o mai" and means "to become". The correct number for the word is 1079 which is spelled "genet e" which means "to birth" not "to become". The correct English translation is more like "and the word was birthed in flesh" which is compatible with "born of a woman" or "made of a woman". Spirit can never "become" flesh. It can come "in" the flesh, and this is what John says later in his first letter, "Jesus Christ has come "in" the flesh. Continuing in John 1 in the same verse it says, "and tabernacled (4637) with us, which describes a dwelling place or house which is consistent with the Spirit being housed in a body. The Spirit didn't become a body; it was housed in a body. "God is not a man that he should lie, nor the son of man that he should repent" (Numbers 23:19 and 1 Samuel 15:29). And great is the mystery of godliness,....., God was manifested IN the flesh....(1 Tim 3:16). And Jesus Christ has come IN the flesh (1 Jn 4:2-3). "Okay, Why so picky about original language and certain spellings of words"? We can't build doctrines on one verse, out of context, wrongly translated. There are many ways to interpret many words and if it is consistent with Jesus' words then we have liberty to express thoughts in many synonyms. However, when one wants to argue the point that the flesh of Jesus is God and that the Spirit became flesh, and God died on the cross, based on one wrongly translated verse, then it becomes necessary to know the original script. God cannot die. He's infinite. That's consistent with the rest of the Bible.

Continue in chapter 1 verse 4 of Hebrews (remember Hebrews, this is a book about Hebrews), "having become so much better than the angels, he has inherited a name (which means character) more excellent than they. He was made lower than the angels (mortal, so that he could die for us, verse 2:9) but became better. Now he quotes Psalms 2 especially verse 7, which sets him far above angels. The Son is not just a spirit sent from God as are the angels; he is The Spirit, The Son, The ONLY begotten Son of God. The Father is the Holy Spirit. The Son is the Spirit, the Holy Spirit. However, The Spirit is Holy and doesn't need to be called the "Holy" Spirit of Father or Son, but when the Spirit is "in" us whose minds and bodies are not holy, the Spirit needs to be called "Holy". The Father is in the Son and the Son is in the Father. God is one. God is a Spirit. "What about the trinity"? That word is nowhere in the Bible and neither is the concept. You can find many arguments about it on the internet, but that's usually the fruit of bringing it up, an argument. It was started as an answer to a manmade heresy that said that Jesus was only an apparition and did not have a physical body; it was labeled "Docetism". We should stay away from men's arguments and doctrines of men, traditions of men that make the word of God of no effect (Mt 15:6). Every denomination was founded on the premise of disagreeing with the previous religious argument. We need to go back to the original, the original language by the original leader of our sect, the sect of the Nazarenes, the Way. Jesus is our Pastor. We are all brothers and sisters and there are real born from above followers of Christ in all denominations and some in no denomination. None of us are the leader. We have one master even Christ. And if you think you are a leader, then serve; be the lowest; be thought of as a servant not a leader. People call us pastors and we may be, but we should be leading by serving, giving our lives for the sheep, not depending on them for our "healthy self-image" or income. I remember one evangelist who loved to travel and wherever he went he would be welcomed and known and revered. He would always have the opportunity to say, "It's all about Jesus, not me". Until one time he went somewhere where they had never heard of him and he felt like, "Hey, don't you know who I am"? And he said, "I at least wanted to have the opportunity to say, it's not about me". We desire to be servants until someone treats us like one. The son of man came to serve, not to be served. (Mt 20:28, Luke 22:27). Sometimes there are words in *italics* in the Bible. This is done when the verse doesn't appear in the oldest manuscripts, in other words it was added later and is really not part of the original Bible. Such is the case with 1 John 5:7. Only four or five of the newest manuscripts, from the fourth century contain the italicized verse. It should read from the original, oldest manuscripts, "For there are three that bear witness on earth......." But someone added, "in heaven, the Father, the Word and the Holy Spirit and these three are one". Check the footnotes in your Bible. This verse is the only verse that says "there are three in heaven", and for those in error, it supports the trinity doctrine. Again, one verse, not in the original text, used to build a whole doctrine.

And when he brought the "firstborn" into the world he said, "And let all the angels of God worship him". Worship the Spirit in the man, not the man. How do we know? When the rich young ruler approached Jesus, he asked, "good master......."? Jesus said, "Why do you call me good? There is none good but one, that is God" (Mt 19:17). He never wants us to worship the flesh of anyone, not even the flesh of Jesus Christ.

Hebrews 1:8, "But as to the Son, "Your throne, O God, is forever and ever............ Your God has anointed you......." So the Father, the omnipresent, speaking to the Son, the Spirit confined to a body, is calling him God and saying that he is the "anointed one" or in Greek, "Chrio" (5548 from 5547 Christos). When God planted the seed, the one cell with all the DNA of the body he made in the beginning, in Mary, it grew. It multiplied by cell division. The one cell containing the Spirit of God split into two. There were two cells but only one spirit in both cells. "Oh, okay". "Wait, ...What"? Okay, there is only one spirit. That Spirit is in both cells just as the Spirit is in you and in me. Same Spirit. It's not physical. It's spiritual. And we may have to chew on that for a while before we get it and that's okay. We are not used to thinking without the physical. For everything we do and everything we think there is a physical representation. But that's not thinking spiritually. The Spirit world is invisible and not physical. This is why Paul says in Colossians 1:15 that Jesus Christ is the "image" of the invisible God. No one has seen God at any time. The Son reveals him, in a body, but it is the same Spirit. There can never be more than one Spirit. Think of the Spirit as the ocean (okay, this is another earthly, physical analogy, so it will lack some understanding but it might help). The vast ocean of water is like Father. If we throw a test tube in the ocean and it fills up, the water in the tube is like the Son and is confined and limited. The tube is not water, only the water IN the tube is water. It may flow in and out but as long as it is in the tube it is confined. There are not two waters. It's the same water. The tube is Christ, the body, and it is filled with the water (Spirit). We, are like test tubes as well having a deposit of the water in us, the Holy Spirit, a small deposit, (maybe like a drop), and even when we are "filled with the Spirit" we are not the fullness of the godhead dwelling bodily like Jesus. Someday, when we receive new bodies, we will be sons like Jesus. He is the "firstborn" of many sons (this is what Paul was referring to in Romans 8:19-23), and by "sons" we mean children, male and female. <u>When we see him</u> we shall be like him (1 Jn 3:2). For now we have a promise, a guarantee, until the redemption of our bodies (Eph 1:14, Rom 8:23). Thinking in the Spirit, requires being born of the Spirit and takes breathing in the words of Jesus daily. I know of no other way. One of the best guitarists ever has said something like, "If I miss a day of practice, I can tell. If I miss two days, my family can tell. If I miss three, the critics can tell and if I miss four, everyone can tell". I think it is that way with us and meditating on his words every day. Others know when we haven't been with Jesus by being with his words. We are all making disciples. We are always an example, either good or bad. Every day is a choice.

1:10, still in Hebrews; "the works of your hands", God working through a body. Please look up all the references in your Bible to the Psalms being quoted here. God spoke through David. He was a prophet. Well, at least Peter thought that David was a prophet (Acts 2:30), and so do I. Peter also thought that Jesus was Joseph's son and therefore a son of David according to the flesh, but he didn't have Matthew or Luke to read. However, to fulfill prophecy Jesus was born of a woman, a surrogate mother (but they didn't know about that yet) and legally an heir to the throne of David according to the flesh because they supposed that he was the son of Joseph (Lk 3:23). Personally, I think God helped this idea along by having the body, Christ, the man, look like Joseph and Mary, the way our children have our features.

Everyone, the good, the bad and the ugly all knew him as the "son of Joseph", the carpenter's son. No one knew of his divine birth, well, except Mary and then Joseph. But Mary kept that secret until; until she told

Matthew or Luke or both and they wrote about it 60 or 70 years after it happened. Even then it was years before these writings were circulated. So we will find quotes all throughout the gospels and the epistles, that Jesus was the son of David according to the flesh, or Jesus of Nazareth, the son of Joseph, but just because they didn't know about his "virgin" birth or Bethlehem doesn't mean it didn't happen. But make no mistake; Jesus the Christ, the son of man was not the son of Joseph and therefore not the son of David according to the flesh. He was not the product of Mary's egg either. That would make him a descendant of Adam and consequently Adam's sin and he had no sin. Jesus called himself the "son of man" because he was born of a woman and told no one of the "virgin birth". His virgin birth is not proof that he is the Son of God; the resurrection is. It is all about the resurrection. This is the gospel. No one preached about the "virgin birth" in the first century and no one celebrated "Christmas" for three hundred years when it was invented. They preached about the resurrection. Mary of Bethany believed him and anointed him for burial and then did not go to the tomb, because she believed him, that he would rise from the dead (read TSW). And what she did should be spoken about everywhere the gospel is preached.

God never spoke to the angels the way he spoke to the Son. This is because the Son can do only what he sees his Father doing. The son is not able to do anything of himself (Jn 5:19). He was not able to sin. The angels are sent to minister because of us, mankind, the ones about to <u>inherit</u> salvation.

2

The Christ

There seems to be a natural break here. I think Jesus, himself, wrote chapter one and after it began to circulate others added commentary. I think others like Paul and Barnabas, maybe Apollos, even Aquilla and/or Priscilla ("A woman? Sure why not, they're equal in God's eyes, read TSW) added exhortations for the readers, and then when it was compiled as one "letter" it was translated into "proper" Greek. Nevertheless, there is a natural break here even though the original letter didn't have chapters and verses. The main point is salvation. Salvation or redemption will always be the main point. Jesus is always pre-eminent and there is salvation in no other. His suffering and death, the blood emptying out of his body, bought our salvation. He tried to explain this to his disciples when he showed them the keys to the kingdom. We have the keys to the kingdom, the keys to freedom but sometimes we either don't know what they are or how to use them. In Matthew 16, Jesus tells his disciples, "I will give you the keys to the kingdom of heaven, the keys that open the kingdom of heaven to us right here on earth. He then describes what to do with these keys. We can't unlock anything on earth that isn't already unlocked in heaven and we can't lock things on earth that aren't already bound in heaven. "Your will be done in earth as it is in heaven". "Like what"? I don't know for sure. But I don't think we have control over anyone else's forgiveness or redemption. We know what John 20:23 says, however, only God can forgive sin. We can forgive someone or withhold forgiveness but that only affects our spirit life not theirs. When we are born of the Spirit if we have unforgiveness, it stunts our growth not the other person's. Before we are born of the Spirit, it really doesn't matter, we're not even born yet. Jesus went on to "show" them that it was necessary for him to suffer and to be killed and from the cross as he was dying he forgave them. He was "giving" them the keys that open the heavenly realm here on earth. This is why the apostles rejoiced when they were beaten, because they were using the keys to the kingdom. When we suffer unjustly and forgive we enter into the spirit realm. It will never make sense to the natural minded man. Peter, in his first letter said it this way, ".....if you are suffering doing good and patiently endure, this is a grace from God. For you were called to this, for even as Christ suffered on our behalf....."(1Pet 2:18-25). All our suffering won't save anyone but it makes an entrance into the heavenly realms for us here on earth. Only Jesus' suffering and death saves us, because he was the perfect sacrifice. His words are Spirit and Life. His word will never perish. His character, or his name, is the only name given for us to be saved. For this reason, we ought to give our undivided attention to meditating on his words, "the things heard" that we not slip away at any time; that we not drift.

Have you ever been to the beach and gone out in the water for a while and noticed that the umbrella where your family is staying has moved? Well, of course it didn't move but it seemed like it. Without noticing, unless we are deliberately staying on track, we drift, just like the pull of the current. Paul tells the Ephesians in his letter to the church that the course or current of this world is full of disobedience, lusts and the will of the flesh..... (Eph 2:2-3). Coasting is not an option. We are either growing or drifting and drifting is moving in the wrong direction. Like a GPS, God is constantly rerouting our course if we miss the last direction, he gives us a new one all the way to the end. We may arrive in heaven and hear, "Welcome son or daughter, we've been expecting you, it's too bad you didn't listen to my directions on Earth, life would have been a lot more pleasant for you, but you're here now, so rejoice. There is a story, and it may be old now and I hope not over used. The story is about Luigi from Italy in the early twentieth century when streams of immigrants were coming to America, the land of opportunity. Luigi saved and saved and finally bought his ticket to come to America on the ocean liner. He brought his salami and cheese and hard bread for the journey. Every day he would pass the dining room and see the rich people eating and he mused, "Someday when I'm rich, I will be in that room. As they disembarked the staff bid them farewell. The maitre d' asked Luigi if they had done anything to upset him or offend him. He said, "No. Why"? The maitre d' said, "Why did you never eat with us in the dining room"? Luigi said, "Well, I just bought the ticket to get me from one place to another. The maitre d' said, "Let me see your ticket. No", he explained, "you could have eaten with us the whole time"! Some are saved but don't grow, living a life of pain and torment. We can have a victorious, abundant life now in the Spirit. Our physical circumstances may never change but we are free on the inside and no one can touch that. "…..everyone that is born (our spirit) of God………the evil one does not touch him" (1 Jn 5:18). Even Satan himself can't touch our new life in the Spirit. We're either growing in freedom or becoming more bound. It is possible to neglect salvation. Once we are born of the Spirit and bear fruit of the Spirit we are sealed with the Holy Spirit of promise. We are saved. We have eternal life. It's eternal. No one can take it away. Satan can't steal your salvation. God will not revoke your gift of "eternal" life. "Neither death, nor life, nor angels, nor rulers, nor powers, nor things present, nor things to come, nor height, nor depth, nor <u>any other creature</u> (whoever they are) will be able to separate us from the love of God in Christ Jesus, our Lord" (Rom 8: 38-39). However, ……. you can drift and there are consequences in the earthly realm, not punishment, (remember he took ALL our punishment). We can obey and grow in Spirit and have abundant life in the Spirit here on Earth or we can drift and lead a miserable life in the physical realm especially if we think that our hope is only in this life (the cares of this life; thorns, just making the voyage, getting from one place to the other) (1 Cor 15:19). If we don't deliberately meditate on God's word, we will be sucked into thinking like the course of this present world. And then, "how shall we escape if we neglect so great a salvation"? Escape what? The consequences or the word here is "payment or repayment" for our actions. We may neglect salvation and not value a new life in this world but God never neglects salvation. His Word never comes back void (Isa 55:11), "…..it shall accomplish that which I please….." And what he pleases is his will and his will is that none of us should perish (1 Pet 3:9)("us" who? "Oh, just our church", I kid you not. Some actually believe that). We shall all come to repentance or metanoia which means to change our thinking. God is our redeemer; that's who he is and what he does; it's his character. What if God is more merciful than we think? Or could ever imagine? He will lead every human being, (not angels nor devils nor brute beasts, nor any other creature) to his way of thinking and he will accomplish his own will. (I know that our Calvinist friends believe that in 1 Pet 3:9 the "us" that is spoken of in "longsuffering toward us" also applies to the word "any" (meaning any of us) and so their logic is that God doesn't will that any of us perish. Further, they think that the "us" is only "them" and maybe some of us, or in other words, only the ones who are already saved and definitely not all mankind). I don't think that Peter meant that God is only longsuffering for those of us who are already saved and withholds his love in longsuffering from those who are not yet saved, which if all things are possible with God could be the entire human race. Our great physician does not have a "DNR" clause (do not resuscitate). He will resuscitate his creation, mankind, whom he loves. He will redeem us. We had a choice in Adam in the beginning and we committed spiritual suicide. We were dead in trespasses and sin. But God provided for our "resuscitation" and will not let us die twice. There are "animal like ones" (or "psuchikos", without spirit, 5591, Jude 12-19) for whom there is no redemption, but animals don't go to "Tartarus" (only used one time meaning a place that is only for angels that disobeyed, a place of torment and judgment). Animals, mammals without God's spirit just die. But the Greek and Hebrew words for death have been translated "hell" and are misleading. Hades means death and Gehenna means death, ceasing to exist not eternal punishment. When we are physically born into the world we are without God's Spirit; we are spiritually dead or spiritually no more than a mammal. God puts his Spirit in some and they become his sons and daughters. They have a desire to please Father. The others that don't receive his Spirit are just mammals, intelligent mammals, but nevertheless mammals and when they die, they go to the grave, that's all. They don't "burn in hell". Those are scare tactics and won't bring salvation to anyone. Christianity is born of love not scared into obedience. "What about the old covenant"? I don't know. I'm just glad there's a new one. And God's word is always confirmed to us by the ones hearing (verse 3). Faith comes by hearing…..hearing the Word of God. Afterward God may bear witness with outward signs but the initial confirmation is hearing God's Word. I hear many looking for confirmation to something they thought God told them. And by the way it doesn't matter if you found gold tablets in your back yard or you think that you are God's prophet or prophetess, if what you are saying doesn't match what Jesus said it's out. Sorry, there are no lone rangers with revelation and hot lines to God. There are no private interpretations. There is only one way to know that God told us anything; that is if it is the words of Jesus or agrees with the words of Jesus. "Glenn, this sounds like you only follow Jesus". Uh, yes, I am a "Christian", a follower of Christ. And confirmation will be hearing Jesus' words, not external signs. External signs may or may not come. But be not deceived; do not be led by external signs. Satan is full of them. He's the deceiver and you are no match for him. Christ defeated him, so we rely on Christ's words. When we are weak, he is strong. "Wait, Glenn, who are these animals you speak of? You need to explain this more"! We will, more in this book later, and especially in our next book specifically on that subject.

In verse three of chapter two we see the phrase, "confirmed to us by the ones hearing". And so I agree with most commentaries that this probably means that the one writing this was not one of the original twelve or maybe even the seventy or the hundred and twenty. The one writing this heard from one or more of the original ones to whom Jesus spoke, "the ones hearing; God bearing witness with them by both miracles and wonders, and by various works of power, even by distribution of the Holy Spirit, according to his will.

It is noteworthy here to bring up the same question that keeps coming up because the concept of three or trinity has been so ingrained in our minds and perception. "Distribution of the Holy Spirit", what does that mean? And the question behind it, "If there is only one God and he is not three of anything then why do we hear the same, "Father, Son and Holy Spirit" phrase to describe him? Jesus himself said to baptize in the name of the Father, Son and Holy Spirit in Matthew 28:19. Red words, Glenn! If there are not three then why keep referring to three"? These kinds of questions lead us to dig and study and ask God for real answers that we will find if we seek. The simplicity of the statement, "Father, Son and Holy Spirit", is that Father is omnipresent, everywhere all the time, the word "Son" expresses Father's reproduction of himself but not separate, confined to a body, not everywhere at the same time and only in one body, the ONLY begotten Son of God. When Jesus was announcing that he would "Go", he said that he would send another comforter, the Spirit of Truth, the Holy Spirit, and then he said, "I will come to you" (John 14: 16-18). In these two verses we have the whole explanation. Jesus, the eternal Son in the body, the Christ, the ONLY mediator between man and God "will petition the Father and he will give you another comforter that he may remain with you forever: the Spirit of Truth........he is with you but will be in you. I will not leave you Father-less (orphans), I am coming to you". This statement is loaded and worded so perfectly as to give us once and for all the meaning of "Father, Son and Holy Spirit". Father is omnipresent, Father as Son is confined to a body, and Father as Holy spirit refers to the Spirit of the Son, the Truth, (remember Jesus said, "I am the Truth" in verse 6) in the ones he would leave behind. So it is the selfsame Spirit IN different physical manifestations, but God is not physical. Father is Spirit with no physical hindrances. The eternal Son is confined to a body and limited (by his own choice Phi'p 2:6-8), "and took the form of a slave", not omnipresent, or omniscient, for he learned, one who knows all doesn't learn, and not omnipotent or all powerful even though at one point he said all power was given to him, (Mt 28:18, the word power here is not 1411, dynamis but 1849 exousia, meaning authoritative power not physical power as "omnipotent" from 2904, kratos, which means strength, power, mighty). The third description of God is in his people. The "Holy Spirit" is a term to describe God's Spirit in a body that is not yet redeemed, that is not yet holy. Someday our minds and bodies will be holy but for now just the spirit is holy. Jesus' mind and body were without sin, holy. So when we say the "Holy Spirit", we don't mean, everywhere always, or confined to his ONLY begotten Son, but in his people (he will be in you), i.e. the distribution of the Holy Spirit. So "baptizing (totally enveloping) them in the name (Yeshua or Jesus or the character of God) of the Father and of the Son and of the Holy Spirit. The name of the Spirit of God is his character, "YHWH saves", and is the character of God (his name is "I am that I am", my essence, my character) whether he is everywhere, or confined to a body or distributed to many bodies (as a deposit, not the fullness, yet). How is this baptism done? How do we immerse others in his name? By being an example of following Jesus' newest and most powerful command, the command that contains all other commands, "Love one another, as I have loved you", by THIS, ALL men will know that you are my disciples"(Jn 13:34-35). That's how we make disciples. That's how he made disciples. That's how we TEACH them to OBSERVE his commands, by them observing us keeping his commands, namely to love one another as Jesus loved us. Jesus' last words in Matthew 28 are full of depth of meaning and invite us to dig a little deeper than what is on the surface. And then he says, "I̲ am with you always". It's ironic. The very teaching that Jesus gave us to unite us, teaching us to let them observe how we love one another and are united by being immersed in his character, has turned out to be one of the most divisive doctrines we have, namely baptism in water and how to do it. Every denomination or call it what it really is, a division in the body of Christ, has its own formula and tradition of what to say and how much of your body has to get wet. Some even saying that without this holding your breath (or nose) under water you can't be saved. Others just say that without this total immersion you're disobeying Jesus. Roman Catholics still maintain that the sprinkling of an infant in salt water is enough to save him. All these people think that their way is the right way. The Crusaders would grab Muslims buy the hair and put a sword to their necks and tell them to be baptized in water or lose your head. And they thought their way was right. And some of you think the way your church does it is the right way. Jesus never baptized anyone in water. He baptizes in Spirit. Paul regretted that he baptized a few in water and said, "Christ did not send me to baptize but to preach the gospel" (1 Cor 10-17). There's nothing wrong with water baptism, unless you think it has the power to do something and that it's required. It's just a ritual, a harmless tradition, unless you guilt people into doing it to be saved or obedience.

The coming world may be like the world before sin. It will not be under angels, but man. We're in Hebrews 2:5ff (and following) now. "What is man that you are mindful of him"? God's mind is full of man, mind full. God created man for a love relationship and gave us the option to respond to his love or not. Adam failed. We all failed in Adam, and "by one man sin entered the world (Rom 5:12ff), ...so also by one accomplished righteousness toward all men to justification of life. .... grace abounded more"! Jesus' sacrifice paid for all mankind; man was given a second life, a new life. Whether we receive that life now or in the end is our choice. Personally I don't see how anyone could resist the love of God, and not respond in like kind. I do realize that sometimes it takes a long time, but then God is longsuffering. Right now we don't see man ruling over anything, we're like pin balls being bounced off of every obstacle that Satan throws at us. Then we are born from above and have a new master, not a slave to sin any longer. But the rest of our lives are spent living in Satan's world with Satan's rulers and being given plenty of opportunity to "overcome". Interestingly, in the first three chapters of Revelation there are messages to the angels of the seven churches. And there are messages to the churches. Every time it says, "Hear what the Spirit says to the churches", it says, "To him who overcomes…..". That is what we've been given power to do, overcome, not avoid, ignore, deny, make excuses for; overcome. The consistent message in all seven churches is overcome! We don't see all things subjected to us, yet, but we do see Jesus who also was made lower than the angels, flesh and blood, so that he could take our punishment, our death sentence for us.

This man through whom all things were made, this immortal person became mortal to bring many sons to glory through his suffering. He is not ashamed to call us his brothers and sisters. We are all born of one Spirit. He is never disappointed in who we are, because who we are is what HE did; we are spirit beings in bodies. He birthed us. We are not our bodies, although the sway of the world would have us believe that. We are spirit beings, born of the Holy Spirit and our minds are being renewed and our bodies are being transformed but we won't achieve the redemption of our bodies until we see him (Rom 8:23, Php 3:20). Then we shall be like him. Who we are, spirit beings, sons and daughters of God, born from above, born of the Spirit, in a body, is what God did. We have been immersed in his Spirit (Jn 1:33). He is never disappointed in who we are, because that is the work of his hands. He is never disappointed, period. In order to be disappointed, he would have had to be expecting something else and God already knows what is going to happen. He may be displeased with what we do or how we think at times but never displeased with who we are. He loves mankind, made man for a love relationship, and redeemed him for such. God is love but he only has a love relationship with those that are born of the spirit; the rest is just dust and to dust it will return. The spirit lives forever and will receive an immortal body. He only accepts his children, those who are born of him. His love is unconditional but his acceptance is conditional. The good news is the conditions of his accepting us have been met in Christ for us. So nothing depends on us. He did it all. And it is finished. It's a gift, and the gift is for everyone. The conditions of acceptance have been met for everyone whom he foreknew. At some point, maybe in the fox hole or at the end of life, I believe every real human will change his thinking (repent; metanoia) and be redeemed because that's God's will. "Well, what in the hell is hell for then"? It was created for the Devil and his angels. Then there's the natural brute beasts that Peter (2 Pet 2:12) and Jude talk about. There are monsters among us. There are wolves in sheep's clothing. And there are "neutrals" for lack of a better word, just intelligent mammals among us that are not born of God and never will be but they are not going to Tartarus either. There are devils, Judas was one (Jn 6:70), and Jesus said that the Jews were of their father, The Devil (Jn 8:44). There are angels and powers and other creatures (Rom 8:39). When we say mankind, it excludes these other creatures and beasts that look like people but aren't. "Glenn, that's heavy stuff, like sci-fi, and spooky! And I don't believe it"! I know. But all we're really saying is that God loves mankind and has provided redemption for all of mankind, those that in his foreknowledge he knows are more than mere mammals that he will put his spirit into, and eventually the all-powerful God will cause all of humankind to change his thinking (repent) because of his undying love. This is his doing. The Son gives life to whomever he wills, in Jesus' name, and his name means God Saves. That's who he is and that's what he does. I just happen to believe that it is God's desire that all of humankind be saved. I think that he is far more merciful, gracious and forgiving and at the same time more just than any of us or that we have ever imagined. The good news is that nobody we know is going to burn forever. Those of us that are born of God will spend eternity with him. Those of us, that are not born of God, excluding devils that look like us, will just cease to exist like other mammals and won't know the difference. "We won't see some "people" in heaven"? It won't matter then, we will understand and we will not be watching people burn in "hell".

Continuing in verse 14, evidently the Devil <u>had</u> the power of death, but it didn't start that way. In the Garden of Eden, Adam was created to live forever. When he relinquished his dominion over Earth and gave it over to Satan by obeying him, Adam died spiritually and the Devil acquired the power of death over mankind. We discuss "in the beginning" in AV and TH. The point here, however, is that the Devil "had" the power of death. We <u>were</u> subject to slavery to sin by fear of death, but we have been set free. Because God chose to take hold of the seed of Abraham, he could be <u>like</u> us. God could have visited us in the form or manifestation of an angel. He did this in the past through Melchizedek. He could have descended from heaven in a glorious appearance and taken control of everything and kicked Satan to the curb. But he didn't want to control mankind, he wanted to love man. We should be careful of our earthly relationships; are they control or love, they can't be both. God chose love. He chose to be birthed in what was <u>like</u> sinful flesh. He chose to take on the form of a servant or slave in the likeness of men. He couldn't be the seed of his creation, but he took on the form that made him look like the seed of his creation. His earthly tabernacle, house, looked like ours. Looking like us helps us receive him, well, helped some of us, some are still trying to figure it out and God is longsuffering not wishing that any of us should perish. I still have family members who don't know him. How about you? Yeah, it's tough. But he reached me and I have faith that He can reach them. He was able to help me and is able to help them because he came in the likeness of sinful flesh. Not because he wasn't able before, but this is his plan to save all mankind. His suffering helps us, not him. He could have commanded our obedience and loyalty with the ultimatum of obey or hell. Some think that's the way it is now. But it's not. We disobeyed. We deserved the grave, Hades, but Christ paid; he died; he went to Hades and took the keys to Hades and death and gave us freedom when we want it. Hell was created for the Devil and his angels, not humans. I would talk about hell but I think we'll be covering that in the next book, (the title might be something like, "Angels, Demons and Natural Beasts, Who Are They?"). God is able. All things are possible with God. Becoming like us didn't make him able; this was always his plan from the beginning, the beginning of the creation of God. In Adam, mankind chose to reject God. This was necessary for a love relationship. Love gives choice. Now, God redeems mankind; it's not a matter of choice this time. "Well, then you're saying that God forces people to go to heaven". Yeah, think about that one. I don't believe that any real human will burn in hell forever. I believe all real humans will come to repentance either now or the end of life. "What about suicide"? I believe Jesus died for that person and upon seeing a real hell, he wouldn't feel forced to go to heaven. "But won't some be surprised that they are being sent to hell? Like, 'Depart from me; I never knew you'; and those were church goers"? Jesus never knew them; he never had a relationship with them; they were not real people. These are demons that are still arguing with him. These were workers of iniquity the whole time. Everything they did even though it looked religious was a fraud. These are the goats in Matthew 25. These are not humans but imposters among us, frauds, goats, devils, wolves in sheep's clothing. "Whoa! Who can you trust"? Exactly. You can only trust the ones who have consistent good fruit in their lives. In one of the denominations I was asked to leave, the executive pastor said, "Glenn, this would be so much easier if you didn't have so much fruit in your life". Go figure. How oxymoronic. We're admitting that God is bearing much good fruit in your life but we don't want you here. Bad trees cannot bear good fruit. Good trees cannot bear bad fruit (Mt 7:18). More on this later. The point here is that God is saving his creation, mankind. It will take time but we will eventually realize that there are imposters among us. The real humans are the few. The imposters are the many. No matter how we imagine this all works, one thing is clear; God is love and he loves and redeems his creation that he created for a love relationship and his plan will not be frustrated. And the best answer we can give on how God is going to work all this out is, "I don't know". "Are you saying that there are demons in the church"? Well, not The Church but the organization called church.

It's interesting here that he "suffered" and it then says, "being tried" or "tempted", it's the same Greek word but translated differently according to the translators preference. The original language or tongue is 3985 in Strong's, "peirazo", it means "to try, to test or to tempt". Jesus, the man, remember, the man has the same name as the Spirit, was made in the likeness of mankind. The purpose of his physical makeup was so that he could <u>suffer</u>. He <u>suffered</u> death so that he could pay for our punishment according to his own law. This is important. This is the theme of chapter two and following chapters.

Father wanted a love relationship. The only way for that to happen would be for the object of his love, mankind, to have a completely free choice. In order for there to be the real possibility that man could choose wrongly, he would at some point choose wrongly. And the only way to have the relationship restored would be that the wrong would be paid for, and that mankind would be forgiven. Then he that has been forgiven much would love much (Lk 7:47). This is the whole reason Jesus, the son of man, was made less than the angels, to suffer death. Hebrews 2:9 continues, "We see Jesus crowned with glory and honor, who on account of the suffering of death was made a little less than the angels, so that by the grace of God He might taste of death for every son. For it was fitting for him, because of whom are all things, and through whom are all things, bringing many sons to glory, to perfect him as the author of their salvation through sufferings. This is why he "took on" the seed of Abraham (born of a woman, although surrogate, still identifying with mankind). This makes him merciful in our eyes, and is able to help us not because he wasn't able to help us before but now we inherit that help because we see him that suffered, being tried. His trial was suffering not sin. His test was suffering; not being tempted to sin. The man, Jesus, was not able to do anything that the Spirit wasn't doing, spiritually, of course. Jesus ate and slept and had bodily appetites but was never able to be tempted to sin because he wasn't able to sin. "The Son is not able to do anything from himself, except what he may see the Father doing;......(Jn 5:19) spiritually, in the spirit realm.

God provided the Lamb for our forgiveness. God knew when he created Adam that Adam would sin. In God's plan he had already created the body that he would sacrifice for all mankind. God used that body to create Adam and then later to take the woman out of the man and make Eve. (read AV and TH) God created mankind to have a love relationship with him and knew that love would be a choice. Many creatures were given a choice, including the angels, obviously, Lucifer, but only mankind was given a second chance, redemption. God knew Adam, representing all mankind would reject him and provided a plan for his redemption by creating a body for himself long before he created anything else. When that body became mortal in Mary's womb, God made the body for sacrifice for all mankind. The choice that all of mankind had was in Adam and man chose to reject God. But redemption, the second chance, the sacrifice, was accomplished in the suffering and killing of the body God made for himself, the innocent suffering for the guilty. God himself paid the penalty he required for sin by taking the sin of the whole world on to the body he made for himself. God didn't die, but the body he dwelled in did. The Son of God didn't die, but the son of man did. God loves man. We are born into this world with a sinful nature that we inherit from our choice in Adam, the representative of the whole human race, and we are slaves to sin, but we are forgiven and inherit eternal life. That's love. "What if someone doesn't choose to be forgiven"? In the first place, to word this very simplistically, we can't ever judge whether a person is going to heaven or not. It is God's will that none of us should perish and I agree with that. "Are you saying everyone will be saved"? No, one step at a time. I think (okay, I want to emphasize that this is what I think, not biblical fact but what I think based on biblical fact), I think like H. A. Ironside, from his book, *In The Heavenlies,* that it is similar to a man walking down a corridor and having to choose a door to enter. After choosing and entering, then closing the door he sees a sign on the back of the door that says, "Chosen in Christ before the foundation of the world". God knows. We, as a race, the human race, mankind, had a choice in Adam. I'm not sure we could call our redemption a second choice as much as it is a second chance or a second life. God is never surprised. He knew all along that every real human would always choose to be rescued at some point in his life, even at the end of his life. We get to be born from above. God knows who are his, and in this foreknowledge there is predestination. "Are you saying that God predestines people to go to hell"? No. I'm saying that hell was created for the Devil and his angels (demons). There are angels, demons and beasts (2 Pet 2:12 Strong's 2226 and Jude 4,12,19) that all look like people and then there are people. Maybe only demons who look like people go to hell. We can entertain angels unaware, (Heb 13:1) which means they look and act like us and angels of darkness transform themselves into angels of light so we can interact with angels of darkness, demons, unaware as well (2 Cor 11: 15). Again, we will dive into this in our next book, Angels, Demons and Natural Beasts. I don't see how any person could choose hell. I don't see how any person could choose to be engulfed in flames for eternity. "Well, what if they don't know about it? What if they were never told? What if the only example of Christianity was a bad one, like the Crusaders, cutting the heads off of infidels (Muslims) for not being baptized in water"? Well, then that doesn't sound like much of a choice to me. If someone was introduced to the real Jesus and realized that they were given a second chance and not going to hell, why wouldn't they choose Jesus and then see their name on the other side of the door? "Well, not everybody gets it explained to them the way we get it explained to us". And for that you want them to burn? "No, I don't want anybody to burn but if they don't get it explained to them, then it's just too bad". Really? And that sounds like redemption to you? That sounds like God's will, that none of us should perish? I'm glad you're not God. The truth is I don't know and you don't know, but God knows and he is merciful and gracious and loves man, and we can count on that. As Jude says, "He is able to keep us from falling and to set us before his glory without blemish, with unspeakable joy, to the ONLY wise God, our Savior! (Jude 25). "You keep saying and quoting 'us'. Who is 'us', those of 'us' who are saved or every real human"? Yes. "Wait, what? Which one"? Both. I think every real human gets saved. I can't prove it but I like it, It's comforting. "I don't like it". I wonder about you.

3

Hear His Voice

"For which reason.........." I don't think there should be a chapter break here. But there is, so we'll go with it but I think this is a continuation of the reason Jesus came. There has not been a greater man that ever lived. There was none greater than John the Baptist according to Jesus but that all changed when Jesus rose from the dead. Everything changed when Jesus rose from the dead, spiritually that is. Consider the apostle and high priest of our confession, Christ Jesus. He is over his house, whose house we are, if we hold on to the end. He is the true tabernacle, the house of God, but we are his house, the tabernacle of the Holy Spirit of Jesus.

"For this reason.........", again. The Holy Spirit says, "HEAR HIS VOICE"! There are no more important words in the whole Bible than the words of Jesus; hear him! Do not harden your heart. Hear him. Father says, "Your fathers tempted me....." Really? Father was tempted? No. They tempted but he wasn't tempted. "Huh"? Okay, they tempted the Lord but the Lord was not tempted. God can't be tempted. "But he says, "Thou shalt not tempt the Lord". This was Jesus' answer to Satan when Satan tempted him to tempt the Lord. Satan is the tempter, he always tempts but who he tempts is not always the "receiver" of temptation. In other words someone could tempt me to smoke a cigarette but I wouldn't be tempted, but someone next to me who is trying to quit would be tempted. The tempter tempts but he doesn't always find receiver. Maybe James can help us out here (James 1:13-16); Jesus wasn't drawn away by his own lusts; he didn't have any. He never had a sinful nature. He never knew sin. God is not tempted. Satan tempted Jesus on the outside but Jesus wasn't tempted on the inside. The confusion comes from using the same word to describe two different actions. Being tempted describes the action of the tempter to his intended victim, whether the victim feels tempted or not. Sometimes we're tempted without a tempter, such as, "I'm tempted to break my diet and get a big bowl of ice cream". There was no tempter but we say we are tempted. That's because it came from inside. Jesus had no inside temptation. Similarly, one who doesn't like ice cream could be approached by someone trying to tempt him to have some and although he would be tempting him the one being approached wouldn't feel tempted at all, but someone on a diet would. "Are you saying Jesus wasn't tempted to jump off the building? That he wasn't tempted to fall down and worship Satan"? Those are kind of easy to recognize. But what about turning the stone into bread? He was hungry. There was no struggle. Jesus was not tempted on the inside to seek the food that perishes. He is the Bread of Life. He's the one who said, "Labor not for the food that perishes" (Jn 6:27). This is why just quoting Bible verses doesn't make temptation go away. Many have taught that we should just do what Jesus did. He quoted scripture from the Old Testament and the Devil went away. Movies have tried to dramatize this moment but since Jesus had no struggle, since there was never any sinful nature in Jesus to tempt, he just quoted a verse and moved on. Have you tried this? It doesn't work and it's not your fault. Maybe you've been told you don't have enough faith, or you didn't quote enough verses or you should fast or cry or shout at the devil or jump up and down and stomp your feet. People do this. It's a three ring circus. Jesus said, "Watch and pray, that you enter not into temptation". We overcome by the word of our testimony, and by Jesus' death and resurrection (the blood of the Lamb) and by not loving our lives to the death. Jesus quoted old testament verses to the Devil to show that he fulfills the law. We don't. We make the mistake of thinking that temptation is a spiritual battle. "What? It's not"? No. The spiritual battle is in the spirit world and is concerned with being born of the Spirit. We do spiritual battle when we witness to someone who needs spiritual birth. Once we're born of the Spirit, the spiritual battle is over. We are now in the battlefield of the mind. We must renew our minds by the washing of the water of the word. The spiritual armor in Ephesians 6 is for a spiritual battle, "in the heavenlies". That's why the terms have to do with being born from above of the Spirit; righteousness, salvation, truth, the gospel, faith, the Word. Once we're born the battle is all in our minds. All the junk that was deposited there has to be cleansed. The devil is not in you when you're born from above but he's already planted weeds. The Devil can't touch you. "What? It sure feels like he's touching me, torturing me, tempting me". I know. But we're drawn away of our own lusts. And when lust conceives it brings forth sin. So the temptation is not sin but following through is. Thoughts and desires are not sin unless we start planning our actions. Remember James 1? And Jesus didn't have his own lusts. In John's first letter, not the gospel but the letter, chapter 5, verse 18, it says that everyone "born" of God does not sin and the evil one does not touch him. The part of us that's born of God is our spirit, who we really are, spirit beings, and the spirit doesn't sin because it is born of God and the evil one can't touch our spirit, who we really are, that's why it's not a spiritual battle. Instead we need to "gird up the loins of our mind" (1 Peter 1:13ff). We can obey because we are already born of the Word, the incorruptible seed. We are not the slaves of sin any longer; the spiritual war is over for us personally, the only spiritual war we have is when we seek to help someone else connect, that isn't born of the Spirit. Rather, ".....arm yourselves with the same <u>mind</u>"!(1 Peter 4:1ff). "Fine. But what difference does it make, it's still a fight"? Yes, but we're cleaning up the mine field left behind from the war not fighting the war. It's important to know that Jesus has already won the war and we are saved, new, have eternal life and the war is over. We can stop sinning. We may not be sinless but we can sin less. We're just learning how to navigate through the mines, the bombs Satan has planted in our minds. We have to learn how to diffuse and discard these land mines which are thoughts that exalt themselves above the knowledge of God (2 Cor 10:3-6). It's a battle in the mind not a war for eternal life in the spirit. We are no longer slaves to sin. The hardest thing in the world is to try to become something you already are and don't know it. If you are truly born of God, then you are a new creature in Christ, (spiritually) old things have passed away and all (spiritual) things are new (in the spirit realm). But the mind! It needs an overhaul. Jesus never had a mind struggle because he never had the garbage planted there from an old nature, that's why he couldn't be tempted on the inside. There was nothing on the inside to tempt. "So how does that help us then? I thought because he overcame by quoting a verse and he was a man, so could I". Yup. And that's the problem. "Let this mind be in you that was in Christ Jesus; think on these things; the renewing of the mind"; look up verses that have to do with the mind and thinking and there we will be able to arm ourselves, just quoting a verse won't do it. Maybe you already found that out. "Well what's the armor in Ephesian's six for then"? It's to stand against the wiles of the Devil. He can't touch you but he tempts and influences those who are not born of God yet. We don't wrestle with them, flesh and blood but against spiritual powers in the heavenlies. We wrestle for their good. We are used to preach the good news to rescue real humans from death, Hades. We are used as instruments of righteousness to making a distinction and snatching some from the garbage heap of fire (Jude 22-23). "So how do we know who will respond and who won't"? We don't. So tell everyone. Again, it's a privilege to be used not a duty.

Jesus wasn't teaching us how to overcome temptation here, because he wasn't tempted on the inside. The word for tempted and tried is the same (peirazo 3985) and Jesus was tried by <u>suffering</u>, not <u>tempted to sin</u>. He was not able to sin. He was not able to do anything he didn't see Father doing. "So why did he come then"? He came to destroy sin, not relate to it. He came to relate to our suffering, not temptation to sin. We can overcome sin in our minds and actions because "Greater is he that is in us than he that is in the world" (1 Jn 4:4). He that is in us cannot be tempted to sin. Jesus never lusted. He never envied. Riches and the cares of this life never tempted him. "But, he was tempted in all points like as we are". First of all we need to read the whole sentence. "For we do not have a high priest not being able to sympathize with our <u>infirmities</u> (weakness, illness, sickness, astheneia 769 in Strong's ; he felt pain, hunger, tiredness) but one having been tried in all respects according to our 'likeness', APART FROM SIN!" That's in chapter four and we'll get there but first we have to establish the fact that he suffered, that we find in chapters two and three.

Heart always means "center" in the Bible. Please do a word study on that, there are plenty of verses to show that. Our center can get off, we can drift, and that happens when we have unbelief. Evil unbelief isn't doubt. Doubt is not knowing what to believe, hesitation, confusion but wanting truth. Unbelief is the opposite of belief. Unbelief is the refusal to belief even in the face of the evidence of truth. There was unbelief in the children of Israel in the wilderness because they refused to believe in the midst of so many miraculous deliverances. And in John 12 in spite of all that Jesus did that the people witnessed, miracles, verse 37 says, "But though he had done so many miracles before them, they did not believe into him". Unbelief is refusal to believe and it is evil. Doubt is not sin. Continued unbelief for the one born from above could cause him to not see the value of his salvation, neglect so great a salvation and consequently begin to "fall away from the living God". But he is able to keep us from falling (Jude 24). Hearing his voice is the only way to grow and if we are not growing we are becoming dull of hearing. So in the old covenant you couldn't enter into his rest unless you obeyed. And because of unbelief none of the generation that left Egypt were able to enter the promised land, except Joshua and Caleb. They were in the wilderness forty years and their kids inherited the promised land. In the new covenant, Jesus obeys the whole law and if we take his yoke upon us we will find rest, and not just one day a week on the Sabbath but every day; God may be more merciful than we could ever imagine. In the new covenant we obey because we have entered his rest.

4

Temptation

Again, another awkward chapter break. We start with "Therefore". So we're still on the same subject and we can ignore the break. So it is possible to hear without hearing. The hearing that the Spirit urges is that there is evidence of change of behavior. Faith, we will find out later in chapter eleven is evidence and substance. Faith without works isn't. "Isn't what"? Isn't faith. "What is it then"? It's wishing and dreaming and fantasizing. It's thinking about doing something but never doing it, good intentions. Temptation is not sin, but neither are good intentions faith. "Well what about if a man looks at a woman to lust after her? Hasn't he already sinned in his heart"? Yes. The reason is the action of planning, "toward lusting" after her. But just looking and being tempted and not planning is not sin. It was explained to me this way: if a guy sees a scantily dressed girl walking down the sidewalk while he's driving and looks in his rearview mirror he's tempted. If he goes around the block for a second look he's sinning. Now, I'm not sure that's completely true but there's a point there. He has begun to act on the temptation, "to lust". In the same way just thinking about doing something good isn't fruit. It isn't faith. Faith is evidence. Verse two says that they who left Egypt had the gospel preached to them. Indeed, everything in the old covenant points to the Messiah. The problem wasn't that they didn't have a Messiah, because they had the promise of the Messiah, the gospel. The problem was that they didn't have faith. And so it is now. The solution isn't that we have a Messiah, the gospel. Many preach the gospel but have no fruit. The solution is having faith in the Messiah, works, evidence, fruit and actions that speak louder than words, which is why we say, "Preach the gospel and sometimes use words". In the old covenant, God had provided a certain day to enter into rest, the Sabbath. But they refused to obey and thereby enter in. Even Joshua couldn't give them rest just by going into the promised land, even though he had the same exact name as Jesus and some bibles translate it that way, from Joshua which is Yeshua, to Iesous, to Jesus. The gospel doesn't save anyone. It's the Jesus of the gospel that saves. You are saved by grace through faith (Eph 2). And God has given every man the measure of faith to be saved. Every day that we can say, "Today", we have a choice to either harden our hearts or hear his voice. "You mean I have to read my Bible everyday"? No. You get to. And not just your Bible, but specifically the red words or the words of Jesus Christ. We can "hear" God speak to us every day if we want to. He can speak directly to our spirit and guide us into making good spiritual decisions. "What about good financial decisions? What about finding a spouse? What about health"? If we have the answers to eternal life, spiritual answers, then we can apply those principles to making Godly decisions with the cares of this life, like work and have a budget or no sex before marriage or eat what God says to eat and don't eat what God says to not eat. "That sounds legalistic"! Of course it does. Anytime God's word doesn't agree with what we want, it's sounds legalistic.

Therefore let us labor to enter into his rest. Labor isn't a bad thing. Works are not bad things. We just can't earn rest; we enter into it. The word of God is living and powerful and sharper than any double edged sword.......dividing soul and spirit,.......able to judge thoughts and intents of the heart. That's a big verse; it's loaded with meaning and application. But first we have to realize that the word of God is living. Jesus Christ is the living Word of God. He was birthed of a woman and lived in a tabernacle among us. So his words are the word of God. There is a difference between soul and spirit. I think the difference is that the soul is the psyche or the mind, will and emotions. While the spirit is who we are, our being, our new nature, our divine nature, our new life since the old life died. We, the spirit, own a soul and a body and we're working on converting the soul and one day our bodies will be redeemed (1 Thes 5:23). We do this by not conforming to the world, hearing his word which renews our mind and being led by the spirit (word) our bodies are transformed (Romans 12:1-2). I am not my body; I have one but that's not who I am. I am not my mind; I have one but that's not who I am. I am a child of God and so are you if you have been born of the Spirit. A person or one that looks like a person without the Spirit of God is no more than a mammal, spiritually, an intelligent mammal but not a born spirit being. Mammals don't go to Tartarus (hell prepared for the Devil and his angels), they just go to the grave or death (Hades or Gehenna or Sheol). God sees everything I do and knows all my thoughts, and I feel secure in that and he is always pleased with who I am. He may not be pleased with all that I think or all that I do but he is always pleased with who I am and that's comforting. Because of that I want to please him in all that I think and do. And pleasing him could be summed up in one command, the new commandment, "Love one another as I have loved you; Love one another". It includes every other command and having this faith pleases God.

We do not have a high priest not being able to feel what we feel in our infirmities (769 in Strong's meaning sickness, or weakness, not meaning sin, not temptation to sin). He has been tried in all respects according to our likeness <u>apart from sin</u>. There are at least two schools of thought about this verse. One is that Jesus was able to not sin (in other words he could sin but chose not to), the other is that he was not able to sin (no choice, he couldn't). We have to remember his own words, "The Son is NOT ABLE to do anything from himself, except what he may see the Father doing"(Jn 5:19). He is NOT ABLE to sin. He didn't come to relate to our sinfulness but to our frailness, our weakness, our suffering unjustly. He has suffered and knows what suffering unjustly is and can sympathize with our suffering. But that's not all he came to do. He came to empathize with our suffering, not just commiserate or complain with us but to feel what we feel and encourage us to endure because of the joy that is set before us (12:2). "...........But if you are suffering doing good, and patiently endure, this is a grace from God. For you were called to this, for even Christ suffered on our behalf leaving behind an example for us, that you should follow his steps; who did no sin nor was guile found in his mouth; who having been reviled, did not revile in return; suffering he did not threaten but gave himself up to him who was judging righteously"; now this next part we can't do. We can't bare in our bodies our sin, only he can do that, so when we say follow his example we don't mean that we can be perfect and fulfill the law and the prophets, only he can do that. And speaking of righteousness we were healed by his wound. We were forgiven. We were straying sheep. It doesn't say anything about physical healing (1 Pet 2:19-25). I believe all healing comes from God. I believe everything good comes from God. But to say that because Jesus died on the cross, we can heal people is a bit of a stretch. Experience in many different religious Christian circles, Charismatic, Pentecostal, Spirit filled, or nondenominational has taught me that summoning God to heal people at our beck and call, having God "on tap" so to speak is disrespectful to God, misleading to the people and causes many a heart to be sick because of "hope deferred". There's a lot of disappointment in these churches because most people though they believe and fast and pray and pray in the Spirit and kneel and bow and sing and praise and give money to the church and are faithful in attendance and are leaders and even on staff, still experience no healing. And most of the "stories" I hear about God healing through a certain "gifted" person is always overseas somewhere that I can't witness. God heals. And we can certainly ask for his healing, but like Paul we may need to learn about grace. He said to Paul, "My grace is enough for you" and Paul was left with a thorn in the flesh. Let us get close to the throne of <u>grace</u> with confidence knowing this, that we may receive mercy, and we may find <u>grace</u> for help in time of need, because he "gets it". The question we need to ask ourselves is, "Is God's grace enough"? He may be more gracious than we think. Some Bibles say "sufficient". It means the same thing. Is God's grace sufficient, enough? "For what"? For everything; for salvation, for growth. Or do we have to add something to his grace? Grace yields works not vice versa. God's grace has given us the faith we need to be saved. "Well, what's our part then"? We change our thinking. We "metanoia", translated repent but it means to change one's mind. Every time you see repent or repentance in the new testament it is "metanoia", to change one's mind and is the key to being saved. "Repent or perish". Change your mind or your thinking and be saved or after you're saved change your mind, even your belief system, even your theology (unless it's already perfect) and grow. So many church goers that might not even be saved hang on to their doctrine and theology and refuse to change their thinking. The very thing that will get them saved or cause them to grow. Jesus' words will challenge your thinking and cause you to change your thinking. I promise you, you will not grow by memorizing old testament verses and keep repeating them over and over. Hear his voice. This is my Son; hear him! Not Moses and Elijah (Mt 17). The words that Jesus speaks are Father's words (Jn 12:47-50, 14;10, and 23-24). Jesus' words are Father's words and the most important words in the Bible. No one else can make that claim. And yet sometimes it's more comfortable to keep our old ways than to change. Some will say, "Well, I just think that the whole Bible is the Word of God and the red words are just one part of it all". If we don't change our thinking on that we won't be able to think like Jesus. And we can't think like him unless our brains are totally submerged in his words, in his character which is his name. To be baptized in the name of Jesus is to be submerged in his character.

5

The High Priest

Christ did not glorify himself to become a high priest. Father speaking to him said, "You are my Son; today I have begotten you" (Psalms 2:7). And again, "You are a priest forever according to the order of Melchizedek" (Ps 110:4). The priests after the order of Aaron had to be appointed by men, and being of like passions or feelings had to offer sacrifice both for himself and the people. He couldn't take this honor to himself but had to be called by God as was Aaron. Christ was called by God as a high priest after the order of Melchizedek (not the Aaronic priesthood because he was not a descendant of Levi or Aaron and legally, he was of the family of the tribe of Judah), even though he is God's Son, his only begotten Son, he still learned (not omniscient; all knowing) obedience through suffering, who in the days of his flesh offered prayers to him who could save him from death with strong crying and tears, having been heard from godly fear. Christ knew what death meant. It meant that the Christ, the man, the body would be separated from the Spirit. It meant that Christ would be separated from Jesus (remember Jesus is God's name, I know; we're just not used to that). God was in Christ, but now God would not be in Christ and the body would become sin and would die, and would be punished in the lower parts of the earth for mankind's (Adam's) sin, so that no man would ever have to go there.

I think, now remember it's just what I think; it's kind of like the Olympics. Well, recently we watched the Olympics and especially the balance beam. Imagine your child on the beam at three or four years old. You're not going to let her fall. But you will tell her if she places her foot a certain way she could fall. So yes she could fall but you won't let her fall. I think that's the way it is for us. We could fall but our mediator will not let us fall. I know; that's not traditional. And some of you want to see people go to hell and suffer. I wonder about you. It is God's will that none of us should perish (2 Pet 3:9, and remember Jude 24, "He is able to keep us from falling"). Man does have a choice, but it was made in Adam. Man rejected God. Now man has a redeemer, a savior, a mediator and he has paid the penalty in full for every real person. What if God is MORE merciful than you think? This is the Light that lightens every man that comes into the world. There are angels walking among us that look like people (Heb 13:1). There are angels or messengers of darkness that transform themselves into angels or ministers of light among us (2 Cor 11:14-15). One of which came to Paul, a thorn in the flesh, a messenger (Greek word for angel, 32 in Strong's)(2 Cor 12:7). Jesus said that Judas was a devil (Jn 6:70). There are natural brute beasts, whatever they are (2 Pet 2:9-14) (Jude 10-12) and there are "other creatures" (Rom 8:39). I don't profess to know all about these entities; I just know they are among us. But when we speak of mankind we're excluding these other supernatural beings that look like people. God loves man. God created man for a love relationship. God provided a sacrifice for man's disobedience and has forgiven and redeemed man for this relationship. And those who have been forgiven much, love much. I can't help but think that everyone who is a real person, a human being descended from Adam will be genuinely saved and born of the Spirit and that none of these others, angels, dark angels, beasts, animals and other creatures that walk and feast among us will be saved. For God so loved the world, (mankind) ....that the world (humankind) might be saved. Everyone believing into him should not perish (Jn 3: 15-17), and God has given every man a measure of faith (Romans 12:3). So I choose to think that every real person, every human being that God created, that God gave the measure of faith to, that God sent Christ to die for and redeem eventually comes to the light that appears to all men and is saved. I also know that compared to all the beings in the world, these are the few not the many. "Narrow is the gate........and few are the ones that find the way" (Mt 7:14). I know there are angels of light and some dark supernatural freaks of nature among us, and God will sort that out. Hell was created for the devil and his angels, not for man (2 Pet 2). "What about Abraham's bosom, the story about Lazarus and the rich man in hell?" I don't know. I know it's an illustration, a story, a parable, (without a parable he did not speak to them, Mk 4:34) in Luke 16:19. The moral of the story seems to be that Jesus is the fulfillment of Moses and the prophets, not so much a tutorial on hell. Another Lazarus did rise from the dead but they didn't believe him either (Jn 11). They plotted to kill him again (Jn 12:10). I think there is a real hell with torment (Tartarus). I just don't think real people go there. There may be many theological holes in that theory but I find it comforting and congruent with Jesus' character. I don't want to see anyone I know go to a place that burns the flesh off of people I know eternally. I don't think that would make me happy or feel satisfied. I don't know how anyone could rejoice as they watch the flesh melt off of people eternally while they scream eternally. And I don't think that is God's character either. Can Christ save everyone? I think so. "Everyone"? Every real human. "Glenn, you're just way out there, man"! Do you say that because there is someone that you think ought to go to hell? I wonder about you.

Just before the story of the rich man and Lazarus, is another story. We call it the "Prodigal Son". I call it the parable of the "Loving Father". In Luke 15:11 it begins. Upon request the father divided up the inheritance to the two sons and the younger son left and spent all his inheritance on wild living. Later the elder son would reveal that the younger son spent his money on prostitutes. The younger son left his family and moved "far" away and lived a life of sin and physical pleasures. Maybe you know someone like this. Maybe you were someone like this. I was. The son was starving and thought about his father's employees or servants, how well fed they were and contrived a story to get employed by his father. I'll just tell him what he wants to hear, "that I sinned" and maybe he'll give me a job and I can eat. He was starving and knew where there was food. But as he started to make his journey to his father's house, his father saw him while he was still "far" away. The same word in Greek is used "makros" meaning "far" and we may lose some of the meaning in English. The boy went to a "makros" country and father saw him when he was "makros" away. His father was looking for him. Every day. It didn't matter what the reason was for him coming back; he was coming back. I think every real person at some point in his life will want to come back. There are no atheists in the foxholes of war with real bullets. Notice the boy does nothing to "deserve" forgiveness. He has nothing to give. He is not repentant, just dying of hunger. He tries to tell his father what he thinks he wants to hear but is interrupted by his father saying to the servants, "Bring the best robe, and a family ring, and shoes, for my "son" lives again". As bad as his son was and as much as he had alienated himself from his father, father never considered that he was not his son. I think this parable illustrates God's thoughts toward his beloved creation, mankind. No matter how much sin we've committed, he wants to run to us and hug and kiss us as his children and rescue us. Some say we have to be repentant for Father to seek us out. Apparently not. The parable of the lost sheep is consistent right before this story. The lost sheep didn't do anything to be rescued except be lost. And I think this is what angered the elder brother. He was typecast as the religious, legalist, mean-spirited, church-goer, that thinks he's done something to inherit eternal life and "by God so does everyone else". If you say that God is going to save all of mankind because he loves us, someone will object because some people will have done nothing to get eternal life. In that case it becomes a free gift. It is grace. We can't boast anything that we've done. "Yeah, but you have to accept the gift". When? "Well, before you die". Well, what if you receive the gift after you die? "No, God can't do that". Why not? "It wouldn't be fair to the rest of us." The rest of us who? The elder brothers? The ones who labored all day? (Mt 20) Can God not do with his own what he pleases? Who can be saved? "With God all things are possible."(Mt 19:25-26) Nevertheless, Father, let your WILL be done. Your WILL be done in earth as it is in heaven. "The Lord is not slow as to the promise, as some deem slowness, but is longsuffering toward us, not willing that any of us should perish, but that ALL of us should come to repentance.

"Well, why should we preach then, if every real human will be saved anyway"? We can be used by God to help others connect and stay connected. But it's not up to us. "What advantage is there to "getting saved" now instead of "enjoying" life now and then still getting to heaven later"? Evidently you have no idea how tormenting "enjoying life" is here on planet Earth. Ask any addict, whore monger, party animal, they will all tell you that reveling in the cares of this "life" is full of pain. Abundant life starts now for the believer, and he can enjoy living life in the Spirit. It's not automatic. Before getting "saved" you are a slave to sin and you can't stop. After being born of the Spirit, we have a choice and we can stop sinning. Not that anyone could be sinless but we can sin less. This gives us a better quality of life right now. And think of the punishments that are still in place unless we receive salvation. For the woman, her husband rules over her, that's right, it was punishment, and for the man it was sorrow all the days of your life. Those punishments are removed for the believer. The woman becomes equal (read TSW) and the man can live in joy. The child bearing thing and the sweat of our brows was a condition, a consequence, not a punishment and so we still have that. But you can be free now or you can be free later. Now is better. "So you're saying everyone gets saved"? I think every real human being, (not angels, good or bad, not natural brute beasts nor animals or any other creature as Paul, Peter and Jude describe who look like real humans) will be rescued by Jesus because that's what he came to do and it is God's will. That's just what I think and I've only recently come to that. I'm not interested in arguing about it because we will find out soon enough and I'm not worried about what I believe. I have confidence and hope and faith and I have biblical evidence. I will and do share the gospel with everyone but don't worry about whether I saved them or not. That's not up to me and I'm not responsible for their salvation. If you think there is "blood on your hands", you are suffering from "churchitis", the mission trip called "guilt" that most churches are glad to send you on. We are responsible <u>to</u> people, not <u>for</u> them. Preach the gospel and sometimes use words. Love one another, as I have loved you, love one another. Our Calvinist friends would agree that God saves those whom he wants saved. I just happen to believe that he wants every real human to be saved. It's not his will that anyone of us perish and I believe his will shall be done in earth as it is in heaven. "What about Jehovah's Witnesses and Mormons and Seventh Day Adventists"? What about them? "Well, they all say that their prophet or prophetess has heard from God directly and yet they say contradicting things. God can't contradict himself. Right"? True. Stick with the red words. I can't judge anyone else's relationship with the Creator, but I choose to only follow Jesus' words and those that agree and not contradict his words. "But they use the Bible and Jesus' words". I know and cunningly, I might add. Someone could say the same about me. You have to read Jesus' words yourself and meditate on what he said and be consistent. If we look at the original language and look up the dictionary meaning and consider the whole context, we'll be on the right track. I think it's like Peter said, "knowing this first, that every prophecy of scripture did not come into being of its own interpretation......"(2 Pet1:19-20). We have a more sure word of prophecy, the words of Jesus Christ.

The Pharisees were angry, and the scribes murmured saying, "This one receives sinners......"(Lk 15:2-32). This is the whole reason Jesus gave them the parable of the lost son. The Pharisees and the scribes were the "holiness" movement of their day, but Jesus said, ".......don't do as they do!"(Mt 23:3). Don't be a Pharisee! Since God wants to save every person, why should we murmur about it?

Next, in chapter 5 verse 11 we see the frustration of the present author because he wants to delve deeper and has much to say about Melchizedek but he knows the readers are dull, caught up in the cares of this life, choked by thorns (and there's plenty to be caught up in, Christmas and Easter and Valentines and Halloween, birthdays, 4th of July, football, baseball New Year's Eve etc). Are you saying those are all evil? No. What I'm saying is that if you spend more time on the things of this world than you do in the words of God, you will be dull and not able to hear his voice. By this time, after all the teaching and reading and studying they (or we) should be teachers but have need to suck on a bottle of milk again. There's nothing wrong with feeding on milk. Desire the sincere milk of the Word, AS INFANTS! There is something wrong when you have to part the person's mustache to get the nipple in his mouth. All of Jesus' parables have to do with growth. We need to grow up. The biggest missing element I see in the church today is maturity. I don't mean age, I mean maturity. I mean taking responsibility for our own actions, not blaming anyone else for our disappointments. I mean freedom, not trying to control the congregation. I mean unity instead of the division of denominations or as they want to be called now, movements; they're still divisions in the body of Christ that should not be so. How is it that we end up exalting ourselves as "leaders"? Leaders should never be exalted. Jesus said that if you want to be leader then be a servant, be thought of as a servant not a leader. Welcome to the "Leaders" conference! There's no such thing. It's immature thinking. It's milk for babies. "Well, we just want to recognize each other. We want the praises of men. There's nothing wrong with taking a little pride in what we have accomplished. It's only natural". Well, that last part may be true.......only natural. But know this, babies are not skilled in the word of righteousness. So is the writer saying that he is mature and not a baby and a real leader/pastor/teacher? Probably. Is there something wrong with that? "Glenn, are you saying that you are mature and not a baby and a real leader/pastor/teacher"? I'm saying that I'm not a baby, but I have a long way to go to get to the maturity of the writer of the fifth chapter of Hebrews.

6

Forever

Before we can begin to comprehend "forever" we will have to leave infantile thinking and milk and mature to solid food. We don't want to keep going over the foundation with doubts and questions. We want to settle some basic things once and for all. That doesn't mean we don't talk about it, just that we have established our foundation and can move on and build on that, not having to go back and question what we believe. In order to do that we have to know what Jesus said. We have to know what Jesus meant. We have to know what Jesus was thinking. And all that information is available to us because he left us his words. Lastly, we have to know him. I say lastly because we have to know what he said to know him. Once we know his character (his name) then we can know him.

Therefore, leaving the discussion of the first things of Christ, let us be brought to full growth not by laying aside or casting down the foundation again but by establishing it. We shouldn't forget repentance from dead works and faith toward God, or baptisms or teaching or laying on of hands or the resurrection of the dead or eternal judgment just because we are leaving the discussion and moving on. We should judge these things eternally not be eternally judging what we believe. We should settle these things. Denominations fight over this stuff and have church splits and divide and think that the "other" church is in heresy. Well, of course, because heresy is anything you believe that I don't. So every denomination believes that the denominations that don't agree with them are in heresy. Some believe that the other denominations are all going to hell (and in the proverbial hand basket). I think we ought to stop talking about who we think are going to hell and probably stop telling people to "go to hell". So it is possible, and here we are being urged, to grow, mature, and move on beyond the basics. Keep them, build on them but don't stay there, sucking milk. I'm reminded of an obstacle course. If someone wants to conquer the course but has only seen the first obstacle, he will only be able to practice the first step. And though he practices every day and can breeze through it with ease, when he gets to the competition he finds that there are seven more obstacles that he knew nothing about. Not only that but there was another group after that and then a final group that contained four stages of seven obstacles. He will always have to be able to go through the first basic step and never forget how, but there is so much more. There is always more. And the more we know the more we should grow and growing means changing.

Now the hard part. Just a couple of weeks ago I would have had all the answers for this difficult part of chapter 6. I've never heard it adequately explained. Preachers, teachers and theologians stumble all over it trying to keep to some kind of concrete doctrine. But like the theory of evolution, the evolutionists disagree and "prove" the other evolutionists wrong. And when we disagree it seems to some that we "prove" each other wrong, so then there is no right or absolute. Recently, I have seen an extremely gracious God who would do anything to keep us from falling. He would risk all for us, his pearl of great price. His plan is to save mankind. So he did. This is hard to swallow, especially if we've been "Christians" for forty years and have always just assumed that people are going to burn in hell for what they've done. Not us though. Somehow we don't have to suffer punishment. Maybe their sin was greater. No, that's not it. Maybe I'm just a better person. No, that's not it. Maybe I just have fertile ground and they have thorns and stuff, like Jesus said. Maybe I just got lucky and I've been predestined to heaven and they've been predestined to hell. Whole denominations believe that. And some very smart, well versed people believe that. Some of the great preachers of last century believe that. I believe that Jesus, our great shepherd came to save the lost. All of the lost. I believe he died for every real person. I do believe that we are predestined according to his will to be saved and spend eternity with our loving Father. I don't believe that our loving Father has predestined some of us, whom he created to have a love relationship with, to spend eternity having the flesh melted off of our bodies, screaming in tormenting flames while he watches and has joy, which would be against his will. Hell was made for Satan and his angels. God is more merciful than we think. And while we contemplate the ramifications of thinking that way, we have these next verses to try to understand. Phrases like, "those once enlightened.....tasted of the heavenly gift......partakers of the Holy Spirit......tasted the good word of God and works of power", and then, "falling away? Impossible to renew to repentance"? What? "But not you" (verse 9).

One thing is clear. Christ died once. There is only one salvation. There is no such thing as "backsliding" and "getting saved multiple times". Christ died once for all. All. So, if it appears that someone has been "saved" and they have fallen away and then come back and got saved again, that's not what happened ; that's impossible. "It is impossible to renew them to repentance for they would be crucifying to themselves the Son of God and putting him to an open shame". "So what happened then"? There is only one salvation. There can be many attempts but only one baptism in Spirit, only one born from above experience. As in natural pregnancy, there are many attempts to bring forth a child, but a child can only be born once. He can't go back in the womb as Nicodemus has pointed out. "What about being born again"? Yes, the word there in the original language is born "from above" (509 in Strong's). One of the things this passage is saying is that there are no multiple salvations for one person. We can be born of Spirit once. I think that the plants that the author speaks about after this sentence in verses 7-8, are twice dead, plucked up by the roots, and cursed and though it rains on the just and the unjust which is a blessing, they are still natural brute beasts, animals, not human at all (Jude 10-18, 2 Pet 2:9-esp 12-22). That's a lot to digest in one sentence. We probably can't discuss this subject in depth here in this book. It requires another book focused on Angels, Demons and Beasts. There have been many books and movies suggesting that there are alien creatures that look like humans that walk among us and we can't tell the difference; and then there's the "Matrix". All this sci-fi has now caused us to dismiss all of it as well, fiction, science fiction. However, if it is a counterfeit, then there is truth about it somewhere.

There are many unanswered questions and we're not trying to, nor can we, answer them all. In all of our quest though, we are endeavoring to know God more. And to know God more, it will always be about his character. We can know about his character by what Jesus thinks and we can know what Jesus thinks by his words. Studying Jesus' actions (what would Jesus do?) and trying to mimic them could be unfruitful at best and maybe confusing. If we try to find a formula for how Jesus acted, it's totally unpredictable. One day he's healing someone in another city without even going there. The next time he makes mud with his spit, puts it on someone's eyes that is blind and tells him to wash it off in a pool that's a half of a mile away. He spits on someone's tongue. The woman with the "issue of blood" just touches his clothing. Jesus didn't touch the one at the pool of Bethesda, but he was healed, but he touched the leper when he didn't have to. So his actions are unpredictable. His character, which is God's character, his name, who he is, never changes. "I am God, I change not" (Malachi 3:6). If we focus on the character of Jesus, the visible image of the invisible God, we can know him. If we focus on what he said, not what he did, it will lead us to what he thought. And we can change our thoughts to his thoughts and thereby renew the mind and grow to know the only true God more intimately and Jesus Christ whom he has sent. We can focus on the faith of those who heard the Word of God from the Word of God, Jesus Christ, the same yesterday, today and forever.

Somehow there is a difference between the "plants" of blessing and the thorns and thistles or plants of cursing. I know some believe that God has chosen some people to go to heaven (plants of blessing) and some people to go to hell (plants of cursing) without having any choice in the matter. I believe that God chooses all people (real people; plants of blessing) to go to heaven. I believe that the only plants that go to hell (Tartarus) are fallen angels among us, that are not real people but only look like people. Far fetched? Well, it's comforting to know that every real person that I know, friends and family will be saved. This "theory" is not against anything biblical; it is based on the Bible. It may not be complete or perfect but it doesn't state that the all-loving, gracious, merciful and just God sends anybody to hell (Tartarus) just because he wants to. I can live with this theology and rest in God's judgment without struggle or hesitation or resentment. I haven't found a suitable argument against it, only those who "feel" like some people "should" go to hell. Again, I wonder about you. For God did not send his Son into the world that he might judge the world (people), but that the world (people) might be saved through him. And concerning who can be saved? All things are possible with God! (Mt 19: 23-26, and in chapter 20 especially verses 14-16, ".....is your eye evil because I am good?). This is what the kingdom of God is like (Mt 20: 1). When we say "all things are possible, it is understood that we mean all things that are not contradictory. The old trick question of, "Can God make a mountain so big that he couldn't move it?" is meant to trick the person into believing that God can't do everything. So it is with God's character. All things are possible with God (with God's character). He can't lie and he can't die; these are not in line with his being, who he is, truth and infinite. But God can save everyone. Mankind has already received the sentence for just punishment for his sin and Jesus Christ has paid it in full. We are left with the consequences of sin, a broken world full of pain and injustice. God is just and merciful. He requires justice and has paid for that justice himself by allowing the body he made for himself to suffer and be crucified. He raised that body from the dead showing his approval of the sacrifice and there remains no more sacrifice for sin. It was once FOR ALL.

We are encouraged in verse 12 to follow those who are inheriting the promises by their suffering and faith, that we not become dull, sluggish, lazy, slow or slothful. When God made promise to Abraham he swore by himself. Abraham received the promise after longsuffering. God gave us strong consolation by two unchangeable things; his promise to Abraham and the hope set before us, certain and sure, Jesus entering into the Holy of Holies, within the veil, our high priest forever, after the order of Melchizedek.

7

Melchizedek

Melchizedek in Hebrew is Malki-sedeq, meaning "My king is just, or righteous". He is the king of Salem (Shalom or Peace), the priest of the most high God, the one that met with Abraham. He is without father, without mother, without genealogy, nor beginning of days, nor end of life but having been made like the Son of God he remains a priest for all time, eternal, immortal, not born of a woman. This is the earthly body God made for himself in the beginning. This is the body in which God visited Adam and Enoch and Abraham. He was called the Angel of the Lord in Old Testament times. This is the immortal body from which God took one cell and placed it in Mary. The difference being that the body born of Mary became mortal for the purpose of suffering and death for you and me. He was able to dwell among us instead of just appearing and disappearing. This body was thirty years in preparation to be the Messiah. This body in its immortal state was Melchizedek, the king of righteousness, the king of peace, and the Son of God (Spirit) dwelled in this body which had now become mortal, a son of man through a surrogate mother, Mary. Jesus Christ is not of the earth, earthy. He is not a descendant of Adam (1 Cor 15:47), he's the Lord from Heaven. He's an alien from heaven. Alien isn't a bad word or a spooky word, it means foreigner. We have legal aliens living in our country. (Well, we have illegal ones too.) They have "green cards" that allow them to live and work here even though they are not citizens.

In Greek it's "paroikos", 3941, translated, "alien, foreigner, stranger. In Ephesians 2:19 we are citizens of the household of God and not aliens or strangers. In 1 Peter 2:11 we are called aliens or strangers (3927) to fleshly lusts. Or, we may be alienated (526) as in Ephesians 4:18. In Hebrews 11:13 the heroes of faith are called aliens. I say this to get us used to using the word "alien" without a sci-fi, spooky connotation. It just means foreigner, a citizen of another country. We were citizens of earth, alienated from heaven; but now we are citizens of heaven and we should feel like aliens to earth. This is the main reason that the "church" should never be like the world. But somehow, someone, somewhere thought it would be a good idea to be just like the world to "win" some. Win some to what? Worldliness?

Consider how great a man this was. Abraham gave Melchizedek a tenth of all his spoils. In the law that followed, Levi would receive a tenth from the other tribes. While Levi was still being thought of in the loins of great grandfather Abraham, (Abraham, Isaac, Jacob, Levi) he gave tithes to Melchizedek. If the law had been perfect we wouldn't need another high priest. We wouldn't need a savior, a redeemer if the law could have given us eternal life. Father wanted us to have eternal life with him. He didn't want obedient robots. The priesthood was changed by God himself. The law was changed by God himself (verse 12). God doesn't change but his actions do. His motive all along was to have sons and daughters in an eternal love relationship and he WILL have that. His reason for creating man was to have a love relationship with him forever and he WILL have that. It's his WILL. It's his purpose. It is just because he, himself has met all the requirements for justice. Still want people to go to hell? I still wonder about you. Jesus Christ, Yeshua Messiah, has become our high priest, not by a fleshly command but by an endless life. He is our priest, forever, after the order of Melchizedek, king of rightness, justice. The Lord swore and will not repent, "You are a priest forever after the order of Melchizedek". Jesus has become surety of a better covenant. He intercedes for us. He's the only one who is qualified to intercede for us.........forever. He has no descendants to take his place; he is forever. Holy, harmless, undefiled, and separated from sinners, he is perfect, forever. He is my intercessor; he is your intercessor. No one can take that place. "But we have intercessors in our church"! No, you don't. They may call themselves that but no one is qualified except the Son of God, Jesus the Christ, Yeshua Messiah after the order of Melchizedek, forever. Thank God! I've seen some of those who call themselves "intercessors". Now that's spooky; crazymatic shakers and quakers, gyrating and speaking gibberish. Lest you be deceived, that's not Jesus. It may be psychological, but it's not Jesus. It might not be demonic or it might be, but it's not the ONLY mediator between God and man, the man Christ Jesus. "But didn't Paul say that we should all be intercessors"? He did (1 Tim 2:1). The purpose for us to make intercession is "that we may lead a tranquil and a quiet existence in all godliness and reverence", not to change them. This is God's desire, that ALL men be delivered, because he is the Deliverer. Then Paul goes on to say there is only one God and one mediator of God and men, the man Christ Jesus, a ransom on behalf of ALL. "For a voiding of the preceding command comes about because of its being weak and unprofitable. For the Law perfected nothing". Jesus is able to save to perfection being the Son forever, our intercessor forever, God being more merciful than we could ever imagine.

Right about here is where the faint of heart start to get a little queasy and start looking for reasons to not trust the book of Hebrews, because it seems to be saying that the Law has become obsolete. It gets worse; or better, if you like the new covenant. In chapter 10, he will say in verse 9, "God takes away the first that he may set up the second". If you push aside the epistle called Hebrews you will be hardening your heart against hearing his voice. "Well, but, it's not red words". It agrees with the red words and perhaps at least the first chapter should be red words. "Well, it wasn't in the original canon". And so now this man made canon determines what is God speaking to us and what is not"? The book of Enoch is not in the canon either, yet Jude quotes it and that IS in the Bible. So it is or it isn't? I don't think we can appreciate the new covenant without "Hebrews". A while ago I asked a class if they thought we could know the only true God and Jesus Christ whom he has sent, if we only had the Old Testament and the gospel according to John. I still believe we can. But to understand the new covenant and to continue to grow I think we need "Hebrews". How else can you understand the high priest after the order of Melchizedek? I would never have made that connection and how could any mere mortal make that connection? I think "Hebrews" is more than inspired. I think it is laced with red words throughout. It gets worse, well, better, depending on what side of the fence you're on. Hebrews is going to tell us that the

Torah is obsolete. And upon hearing that some will be gnashing teeth and hissing. The mind is a terrible thing to waste........and sometimes it's just a terrible thing. Oh, to be able to change our minds; to be able to renew our minds; to be able to Metanoeo (3340)! Hosanna!(5614) "Save us" from our own thinking! Also, on a side note, some think that I have said that I believe only the red words are the Word of God. Well, that's close, but I also believe that the words that agree with the red words are the Word of God also,........of course, and Hebrews is full of the words of God, in my opinion.

8

The New Covenant

We start with a summary, the main point of what's been said so far. We have a High Priest who sat down on the right of the throne of the Majesty in Heaven (meaning according to Strong's 2523 Greek, "to be in a position of high status", authority). Again we have earthly terms to describe spiritual concepts but we are beginning to establish that spiritual is never physical. The spiritual can influence or impact the physical but the spirit realm is not physical. There is no physical throne nor is Jesus literally sitting like in a chair. It means he has finished and succeeded at becoming the eternal high priest, our only high priest, forever, the only mediator between God and man, the man (the spiritual body) Christ Jesus. The things of the spirit are invisible to the physical eye, but can be manifested to be seen by the physical eye. Angels are ministering spirits, but they can be manifested to be seen as men, so much like men that we can't tell the difference, (Heb 13:2 and 2 Kings 6:17, "open his eyes" may sound like the servant saw the spiritual army with his physical eyes but he saw the manifestation of that army with his physical eyes, and Daniel 9:21, "the man Gabriel"). The Son of God is God and was manifested in the flesh (1 Tim 3:16). He is the only qualified minister of the holies of the true tabernacle (spiritual), not made with man's hands. The law was only a shadow of heavenly things. We can think of physical manifestations as shadows of the spiritual. Jesus would not have qualified to be an earthly priest for he was legally from the family of Judah and not of Levi. But he has a more excellent ministry as he is the Mediator of a BETTER covenant. If the first covenant was able to redeem man there would be no need for a better one. And so the Lord said, "I will make an end on the house of Israel and the house of Judah", not meaning to do away with them but to finish what he started with them, namely, redemption, restoring the whole house of Israel back to God. Israel did not continue in the first covenant and therefore was never redeemed. In the new covenant God writes his laws in their minds, not on tables of stone, but on their hearts and God says, "I will be their God, and they shall be my people". And "......all shall know me, from the least to their great ones". All? "For I WILL be merciful to their unrighteousnesses, and I WILL NOT at all remember their sins and their lawless deeds. Can God do that? Is it just? They shall all know me? All? He's going to forgive everyone? "For I WILL...", because it's his will and his will shall be done in earth as it is in heaven, in the earthly as it is in the spiritual. He chooses to not remember their sins and lawless deeds. In the saying, "new" he has made the first "old" and it is near disappearing.

The new covenant is not dependent on our obedience, but rather on his sacrifice and his will. Mankind, in Adam, chose to disobey God and mankind was punished and suffered the consequences of that sin. That was man's choice, every man's and woman's choice. We would have done the same. "Oh, not me I would have obeyed; Adam and Eve were so stupid and because of them look what's happened to me". Uh, maybe a little soul searching will help here. We would have done the same. We are mankind. We still suffer the consequences of that sin which is the answer to every "Why does God allow this to happen?", but we can't tell someone that when they are suffering or have lost someone. The best we can do during those times is to say, "I don't know". But that's not the answer we give when discussing God's character and his mercy and redemption. He has taken away our punishment by his own sacrifice and saved us. The first choice was man's sin. There is no second choice only redemption. There is no more punishment for mankind. There is punishment for fallen angels, Christ didn't redeem them. He redeemed mankind; all of mankind, "All shall know me". To those that he says, "Depart from me, I never knew you"; he never knew! They are not part of mankind. They are not human. They are wolves in sheep's clothing, beasts, (these are biblical terms). "But these creatures in people clothing were in the church! They were doing miracles in "Jesus name". They cast out demons! They prophesied and called Jesus "Lord". How can Satan cast out Satan, won't his kingdom fall"? Well, yeah. His kingdom will fall. They were working lawlessness the whole time. "But they're in the church"! Well, actually they go to a church building and have infiltrated the church but they were never part of the body of Christ. "So how can we know who they are"? Just because someone is religious and can quote the Bible doesn't mean they believe the Bible. We've been quoting from Matthew 7:21ff, the verse before that tells us how we can know them, "by their fruits". There are good trees and bad trees. "Glenn, are you sure about all this"? So far. It's biblical and it's what I know this far, but one of the biggest mistakes any follower of Christ can make is to think that his way is <u>the</u> way. None of us have a corner on the truth. All of our theologies will change, hopefully closer and closer to the absolute truth. That's why no denomination can declare that what a different denomination believes is heresy. Well, they can say that, but all that that means is we believe differently. No one can say that because another believes differently that they are going to hell. I wonder about those. They don't know what spirit they are of, like the apostles when they wanted to call down fire from heaven on someone. It's not a matter of belief or discipline or behavior; we simply are not qualified to judge anybody. God is the judge. Jesus said, "The Father judges no one, but has given all judgment to the Son.......The one who hears my voice and believes the one who has sent me has everlasting life and does not come into judgment.......my judgment is just for I do not seek my will, but the will of the one sending me, the Father......I say these things that you may be saved...."(Jn 5:19-34) of course read all in context. The point is we are just not able to judge. Period. So we might as well give it up. I know there is temptation to think we know who's going to hell but we don't. I've heard people, Christians, say, "I hope they burn in hell for what they did to me"! We really need to remove that kind of thinking and speaking from our minds and tongues. "For God did not send his Son into the world that he might judge the world but that the world might be saved through him"(Jn 3:17). What if God is more merciful than you and I?

9

Blood? Why Blood?

The first tabernacle is described in detail in Exodus (Ex 25-31). There are probably more chapters written in the Bible on the tabernacle than any other single subject. It was important. It has hundreds if not thousands of types and shadows of the Messiah. Jesus Christ is the true tabernacle. However, God instructed Moses to build a worldly tabernacle as an illustration of the pattern he saw in the mountain. Jesus is the pattern. Jesus is the example. Jesus is the beginning and the end. Jesus is the be-all and end- all. This chapter is about that. The author of this chapter was well acquainted with the tabernacle in the wilderness and had probably studied the Exodus account numerous times. He uses it as an example, a pre-cursor of the coming Messiah but knows there is not enough time or space to write about this in detail "now". It is interesting; there are many songs and sermons on how "Jesus is my center", "Jesus paid it all", "Make much about Jesus". However, when you start to explain that Jesus' words are more important, that the red words take precedence, there is this strange opposition to feel the necessity to say something like, "Well, I just think the whole Bible is the Word of God". For some reason this causes division in the church. Jesus' words are the words of God and if any other part of the Bible agrees with his words they are God's words as well. Jesus is God. No one else who ever spoke is God. The prophets of old were (past tense) the mouth of God and in times past God spoke through them, but they weren't God either. The only man in whom the "fullness of the Godhead dwelt bodily" was Christ Jesus. He is pre-eminent in all things. He is the only mediator between God and man. He alone bore our sins. His Spirit is the fullness of the Holy Spirit and if you've seen him you've seen Father. When Jesus speaks, it is always God's Word. When anyone else in the Bible speaks, if it agrees with Jesus words then it is God's word. If not, then it's just that person's words or thoughts. "What about Proverbs"? You would spend your time better listening to the Spirit by reading Jesus' words. "What? Don't you think Proverbs is God's word? I think King Solomon's heart was turned from God and he died in his sins. I think he collected these proverbs but most of them have to do with earthly, material wisdom, not spirit wisdom from above. You can memorize the whole book but I don't believe it will help you think any more spiritual than one of the thousands of self-help books out there that only deal with the soul (mind, will and emotions). I think, *How to Win Friends and Influence People* is one of the greatest books of all time but it's not God's word, even though the author, Dale Carnegie, refers to biblical new testament principles. We're talking about Words that are Spirit and Life and only Jesus made that claim (Jn 6:63). Jesus is the Word of God in the beginning. For some reason, most Bible readers think that the whole collection of history and old sayings and prose and poetry and letters mixed in with the Prophets and Jesus words, is God's Word (The Holy Bible). Esther is a nice story but never mentions God once. Moses was a prophet and more than a prophet and certainly God spoke through him in the Law, the Torah (Hebrew; Pentateuch in Greek), the first five books of the Holy Bible. The prophets spoke God's words, "Thus says the Lord". David was a prophet and some of the Psalms are God's word. Jesus is God's Word and certainly spoke his words. Other than that, the rest is commentary. And for sure when Satan speaks it is NOT God's word. When Job's friends speak it is NOT God's word. When Herod or Pilate or Annas or Caiaphas speak, when the Pharisees or Sadducees speak or the Jews or any other unbelievers speak, it is NOT the words of God. The red letters are the words of God. The Prophets words were the word of God, but they are old covenant unless they speak of Jesus. Jesus is the center. Jesus is all. Make much of Jesus. But be careful when you do; it caused controversy then and still does now. And if you say that the Spirit of Jesus is God but his flesh is not God you could be labeled a heretic for denying the "divinity of Christ". There are hundreds of divisions in the body of Christ each thinking that theirs is the "right" one. If Jesus came today and walked among us as he did in his first coming, he would have to overturn the religious system of our day as he did two thousand years ago. The whole point of this epistle called Hebrews is to exalt Jesus.

In verse 7 we see that the high priest goes into the second (tabernacle)or holy of holies alone once a year, <u>not without blood</u>. Why? Why blood? We have a partial answer. God requires sacrifice, the death of an animal to seal the agreement. In the Old Covenant, the agreement was always confirmed by the death of an animal and its blood being spilled proved its death. It was called "cutting a covenant". It's not the blood that's of any value per se. It is the blood being poured out of the body that signifies its death. The death of the animal is the sacrifice. The death of Jesus is the sacrifice, and his blood being poured out is proof of his death. We say there's power "in the blood" but it means "in the death and resurrection" of Jesus. He died and was raised, that's power. In the beginning God clothed Adam and Eve with the skins of animals that were sacrificed for their sin. When Cain killed Abel, God said that the voice of Abel's "blood" cried from the ground, meaning he was dead, not meaning that the red sticky stuff we call blood was actually crying. Jesus when upbraiding the Pharisees said, "......from the blood of righteous Abel to the blood of Zechariah"(Matt 23:35) meaning the death of the prophets. When we say "blood is on your hands, it's not literal, it means you're responsible for someone's death. If you had all the blood that left Jesus' body in a container, it wouldn't help you a bit. His death and resurrection purchased our freedom and made us free. The power that is in the blood is that it signifies that Jesus died. Power comes from resurrection. "To know him and the power of his resurrection" (Phi'p 3:10). We sing, "There's power in the blood", but it's not the red liquid; it's his death and resurrection. It's not that he bled for us; it is that he died for us. He bled when he was whipped. The crown of thorns caused him to bleed. But it wasn't until he said, "It is finished" that the sacrifice was made, and being confirmed by his resurrection.

In the new testament, in the testament of his blood (death)(Matt 26:28, "......My blood of the new covenant......being poured out for forgiveness of sins.), we have the provision for a clear conscience. The law was never able to clear our conscience. Some still struggle now. But know of a surety that the fact is that our conscience is clear. Now whether we feel like it or not is a matter of belief and our thought life. This is why it is so important to renew our minds. This is why we need to change our thinking. We are clear, bought and paid for, finished, redeemed, forgiven of ALL sin. If we realize this we live differently. Our redemption does not depend on our behavior. Some think it does and the struggle to "please" God is relentless. To the one who believes that Jesus paid it all, he is grateful and wants to obey. The one who thinks he must obey to get saved or to keep salvation, the conscience never FEELS clear. To the one who knows he is forgiven of all (past, present and future) sins, he wants to obey in response and the conscience is clear and FEELS clear.

Christ through the greater and more perfect tabernacle not made with hands, that is, NOT of this creation, through his own blood obtained eternal redemption. The blood (death) of Jesus purifies our conscience to be able to serve the living God, something that the death of animals couldn't do. Because of this he is the only mediator of the new testament/covenant. A covenant/testament requires death. Some people refer to a last will and testament, but there is no testament without the death. It can't be in force while the one covenanting is still living. Even with the first covenant there was death, substitutionary death, but only lasting one year. Christ's sacrifice is eternal. We are already forgiven. We are cleansed. We have a cleared conscience. "Well, but, Glenn, I still feel that we still have to ask for forgiveness, and I do and I teach others to ask also". I know. Would you consider just thanking him for what he has already done, namely, forgiving you? And teaching others that? "I don't know, I just feel.............". One day we won't be led by our feelings; one day we will be led by the Spirit, Jesus' words. "Well, I read the whole Bible"! Here we go again. It seems no matter how bound we are, how trapped we are in the trappings of guilt, shame and condemnation in our conscience, we still refuse the truth that makes us free. Jesus is the Truth. He said so. "Well, I just feel like the whole Bible is truth". Never mind.

Having a clear conscience is a big deal. Christ purifies our conscience from dead works. Discouragement, disappointment, rejection, self-pity parties and the like are tactics of the enemy. They are feelings and although feelings are real they are not always truth. You will know the truth (Jesus) and he will make you free. Apart from the shedding of blood (not the blood but the shedding of blood, death) there is no remission of sin. Christ has appeared in Heaven in the presence of God on our behalf even though he wasn't allowed to enter into the "holy of holies" in the man-made tabernacle. Kind of ironic that the spiritual High Priest was not allowed to minister in the worldly high priest's domain. And many times today, the spiritual ministers are not welcomed in the worldly churches. "Well, our church isn't worldly"! (Right. Well your music is. Your sermons are comic relief. And I've seen some of your people during the week, you know, when they don't act like Christians and then there's Facebook and the elections, good grief! Unified, right?)

And as it has been destined for mankind to die and then be judged, Christ once and for all bore the sins of many, and shall appear a second time to those expecting him for salvation. He has been judged with our judgment and paid the penalty. Judgment is over for those of us who have already received judgment and forgiveness and a clear conscience void of guilt, shame and condemnation. "It sounds too good to be true". I know. But the more we focus on Jesus' words the more truth we will have and the more free we will not only be but FEEL. The good news and the bad news is that I am not as merciful as God and sometimes I'm not always aware that he is more merciful than I could imagine.

10

The Will of God

Every year there was a remembrance of sin, past sins. Every year in the old covenant the same sacrifices had to be made and all our old sins and the new ones were brought up again. Don't you hate it when someone says they forgive you but keeps bringing it up? For some Christians, their lives are worse now than in the old covenant. They don't remember their sins just once a year but every day! You talk about a guilty conscience! How can they ever move on? The law at least rolled your sins over for a whole year. You were covered for the year. They would be brought up again on the Day of Atonement but at least you were clear for a year. Today, we in churches are supposed to be free and yet there are some if not most buying the guilt laden messages from pulpits across America that we have "stolen from God", so give us your money. Or go to the mission field or at least send your money or you are disobeying. And last but not least "Get baptized in water or you haven't sealed the covenant of your salvation", kind of like circumcision. I've actually heard people say, "I don't know if I've been saved because I haven't been water baptized, I'm just not ready yet". Ready? Ready for what? If you don't know if you are saved or not there's a bigger issue than getting wet. "Glenn, there's more to Baptism than getting wet"! Oh? What is it? "It's spiritual birth"! It is? "Yes, Jesus said to go into all the world and baptize everyone; red words"! Yes, but Jesus never baptized in water only in Spirit, so didn't he mean in Spirit? "You're confusing me".

Truth has that effect sometimes but it's just exposing the confusion we already have. The point here is still the same. We should be living guilt free lives because he cleansed our conscience and our hearts don't condemn us (1 Jn 3:18-24).

Jesus, the Son of God, the eternal offspring of God, not separate but confined to a body, says, "You prepared a body for me"(verse 5). And, ".......it was written concerning me, to do your will, O God". Concerning the law of sacrifices and offerings, he takes away the first, in order that he may set up the second. Jesus fulfilled the law, every iota and keraia (Jot and tittle) and in so doing took it away, only to leave in its place the rule of all rules, the law of all laws, the new command, "Love one another". "And the Holy Spirit witnesses to us also. For after having said to us before, "This is the covenant which I will covenant to them after those days, says the Lord: Giving my laws on their hearts, and I will write them on their minds; and I will not at all still remember their sins and their lawless deeds". But where forgiveness of these is, there is no longer offering concerning sins (verses 15-18). These are things God will do, not contingent on anything we will or will not do.

The rest of this we can do if we have confidence, if our hearts don't condemn us. Jesus provided a new and living way, through the veil. Now, this is a reference to the tabernacle. There was an outer veil between the outside and the inside and a veil between the holy place and the holiest place. Going past this inner veil was only done by the high priest once a year. Jesus went past this inner veil, not in the earthly, worldly tabernacle but the heavenly because his flesh was the veil. His flesh died and was raised immortal to never die again making a way for his brethren, us to enter into holiest of all as well. This is why we can draw near with confidence to the throne of grace to receive mercy and find grace (chap 4:16). But we have to get past the flesh. His body is just a veil, not the presence of God, not the Spirit of God. Our hearts have been sprinkled (an old covenant term meaning consecrated; sprinkled with blood) from an evil conscience; no more guilty conscience and our hearts have been circumcised, not physically; it's never about the physical and our bodies having been washed in pure water, we have hope because he is faithful. Our physical hearts are not sprinkled with physical blood and our physical bodies are not washed with physical water. It means that we present our bodies as a living sacrifice and are transformed by the renewing of our minds by the washing of the water of the word (Romans 12:1-2 and Eph 5:26). We should be reminding each other about these things as we gather together, wherever two or three are gathered together. This is NOT an admonishment to go to a church building on a Sunday morning and pay your tithes. Well, unless you are under the law of the old covenant and there is a priest after the order of Aaron in the Levitical priesthood that needs to be supported by the other eleven tribes but that would be on Friday night or Saturday before six pm at the temple or synagogue and that would be <u>old covenant!</u> The old and new covenants were never meant to be mixed. We don't add the new covenant to the old. One will be torn, or the wine will be spilled (Mt 9:16-17). We don't add Jesus to our old life. He transforms us into a new life. We are translated into the kingdom of God's Son (Col 1:13). We die to sin and become alive to God. We become new creatures in Christ; old things pass away. "The one stealing, let him steal no more"(Eph 4:28). "Go, and sin no more"(Jn 5:14). The new replaces the old because the old is fulfilled in the new. The whole law and the prophets are contained in this saying, "Love one another, as I have loved you"!

It is interesting that the premise for this next admonition is said after its application by the present author of this part of the letter. Vengeance. Vengeance belongs to the Lord. So why are we pretending to know how that judgment works? We think it's like Karma; like people are going to reap what they sow. "Yeah, that's in the Bible. But I have a feeling you are going to say it's not Karma". Good! Now we're getting somewhere. Let's look at the letter to the Galatians in chapter six. It's about focusing on the temporary or focusing on the permanent. The flesh is temporary; all flesh is as grass and will fade away; be careful how much time you spend making the flesh look good. The spirit is permanent, eternal life, and we can take part in the abundant life of the Spirit right now. These are life principles not instant Karma. My elders growing up used to say things like, "See, God got you for what you said". That's probably as good a theology as, "If you cross your eyes, they'll stay that way". The passage in Galatians is only speaking to a lifestyle principle of focusing on the physical or focusing on the natural, flesh. Still want to get baptized in water? Eat crumbs and grape juice? Make the "sign of the cross" and dip holy water? None of those things are evil or injurious in themselves but they can get our focus off of the spirit and make us think that because we do churchy, traditional rituals we are being spiritual. That's not spiritual; it's superstitious. It's as productive as leaving a Bible on the dash of the car to protect you from an accident. "What ? We do that! That's wrong"? It's not wrong to put your Bible on the dash of your car, but it won't protect you from anything. "But my grandma taught me that".

God's judgment is God's judgment and none of us are qualified or able to speak to that. All judgment has been given to the Son and he has decided to save not judge. So where does that leave us? We should be focusing on saving not judging. I think the writer here is trying to emphasize that you can only get saved once. I agree. As for someone getting saved and then willfully sinning and then losing his salvation.........I don't think the writer has the judgment to speak to that. I'm not sure who he has in mind that has done all these horrible things but he still doesn't get to judge that. He says, "vengeance is mine, says the Lord", but then pronounces vengeance on these people to whom he's referring. "But it's in the Bible"! And it's not God speaking either. Kind of proving the point. When David was confronted with making a choice as to his punishment in 2 Samuel 24:10-14, he said, "Let us now fall into the hand of Jehovah, for many are his mercies, and do not let me fall into the hand of man". David knew that God was more merciful than he could imagine. The writer of this portion of Hebrews was familiar with persecution and being afflicted and imprisonment (bonds). However, in verse 31, he counts it a fearful thing to fall into the hands of the living God, but David knew better. David's experience with God's mercy taught him that it was something to choose not something to be afraid of. It is a merciful thing to fall into the hands of the living God. The older I get and the more I read God's word and the more I experience in the Lord, the more I realize that he is much more merciful than I ever imagined. He is just. But he has satisfied justice by creating a body to die for all mankind and now he is concerned with salvation and mercy and redemption; we call it grace, for it is free and given freely to everyone. The older I get the more I know but the less I know for sure. When I was younger I "knew" everything for sure. "I was so much older then, I'm younger than that now", Bob Dylan. What I know for sure now is that God's wrath and judgment were "finished" at the cross. But his mercy endures forever. He lives so we can live. And his will shall be done in earth as it is in heaven. I used to think that man's will could block God's will, that God would not force man to do anything. The latter is true. He doesn't force anyone to choose heaven over hell. However, no one would choose hell over heaven if they knew. I knew there needed to be choice to have a real love relationship or we would be robots. We all chose in Adam to sin. But redemption is God's will. God has chosen to save mankind and he will. I don't believe upon seeing hell and arriving in heaven anyone would say, "God you violated my free choice, I wanted to burn eternally". It might be more like when we become parents ourselves we are grateful for the right choices our parents made for us. And maybe wish they had made more. "Glenn, I just can't wrap my head around the idea that everyone will be saved". Well, in the first place only those born of the spirit will be saved. Only real humans will be saved, not the natural brute beasts, or demons that look like people. "Yeah, well, I can't wrap my mind around that either. It's not what we were taught in Sunday school". I know. I think we've established that our theology will change if we are growing spiritually, because we don't have perfect theology now. What's it going to change to? I think as we grow in the Lord we will think more like him and be closer to absolute truth. I think we will know God as more merciful not more judgmental; more forgiving than vengeful. "But the Lord said, "Vengeance is mine..........". I know. I think we should leave that alone. He will decide what to do with his vengeance. I think he already has. He said, "I will repay". I believe he has, with his own body and blood. What more do you want? "I want people to suffer, to reap, to get what 's coming to them". I wonder about you. I think in the end we will come to "The Lord is our Shepherd", that he is the loving father to us prodigal sons; that he is Yahweh Saves as his name says. He is able to keep us from falling.

Verses 32ff seem to be directed at times to a single individual especially "you suffered together in my bonds". That should be a clue as to who is writing but it's not conclusive. It sounds like Paul and he is the prime example of imprisonment but I suppose it could be someone else. It reads like it could be taken right out of a letter to Timothy. This person or group of persons had their earthly possessions confiscated focusing on "treasures in heaven", but are being encouraged to not lose confidence. It sounds like the writer is encouraging the reader to hang on because the end is coming soon. "The one coming will come and will not delay", most agree that this is a reference to Jesus. However, Paul refers to one coming before Jesus, the son of perdition, the man of sin. At that time all the apostles thought that Jesus was coming soon, in a "very little". Jesus had said he was coming "quickly" but it was interpreted "soon". Quickly, means when he does come, it will be without warning, quickly, like a thief in the night. Soon means a lot of things but probably not two thousand years. There are many interpretations by many denominations about the "end times". The group I belonged to believed so strongly that Jesus was coming to Mt Sion, which is Hermon, in Israel at midnight on the feast of Tabernacles in 1988 that we sold all that we had and waited on the mountain. He didn't come. So I understand the disappointment. This kind of disappointment has happened to other groups, the Russelites, the Jehovah's witnesses, the Seventh Day Adventists and others that have popped up more recently. They still want to "teach prophecy about the last days". I think we should let it go. No one knows the future. No one. Jesus knows now but he didn't know when he was coming back while he was on earth; he said so. No one knows. We should stop guessing. We should stop basing our lives on him coming "soon". "Soon" has already passed. The apostles thought Jesus was coming any day until thirty or forty years passed and they figured they better write some of this down because he might not come during their lifetime. Here we are two thousand years later. It's better to live like he's coming tonight, but plan like he's coming in a thousand years. We are who we are because of what he did. We are victorious and confident because of his death and resurrection not because we think he's coming soon. We can live holy and confident and productive lives because he lives. The idea of "You better obey 'cause he's comin' soon!", isn't Jesus; that's Santa, "you better watch out". My three year old granddaughter told her seven year old brother, "If you don't make good choices, Santa will tell Jesus". That's funny. But not so funny when you realize that modern Christianity has some similar ideas about Jesus' coming and Santa Claus is coming to town.

11

Faith

I've heard this chapter referred to as the "faith chapter" or "the heroes of the faith" or the "heroes of faith hall of fame". I think they're all appropriate. Many people have many definitions of "faith" and of course I have mine. We all say our definition comes from the Bible and sometimes you've got to wonder, "Are they all using the same Bible"? One recent comment was that faith and belief are two different things. Well maybe in twenty-first century America they are. However, in the original language the same word "Pistos" (4100,4102,4103,4104) is used for "faith" or "belief" according to the translator's whim at the time, but biblically speaking it always means something we know for sure. In our present society if we are not sure we might say, "I'm not sure, but I believe it's this way". We also say, "Have faith" and mean, just wish and hope for the best and trust. In the Bible, Pistos always means something we know for sure. Thomas "believed" when he saw the nail prints in Jesus hands. The other ten needed more proof (and we call Thomas doubting). The other ten didn't believe even after seeing the nail prints and thought Jesus was an avatar until he ate fish. They needed evidence (elenchos, certainty, proof 1650) and substance (hypostasis, being sure, confidence 5287). "Well, Glenn, I don't speak Greek and neither do you; so why do you keep bringing up the original Greek"? Because, it's the closest we have to the meaning of the words used two thousand years ago. If we say, "Faith is the substance of things hoped for and the evidence of things not seen", we are not saying, "Well, we hope so" or "Just have blind faith", or "Just believe what the pope and his priests tell you". That kind of thinking led us into the "Dark Ages" and the times of the "Spanish Inquisition". Martin Luther put the original sayings of the Bible into a language that the ordinary man or woman could read. He was persecuted for it. William Tyndale was imprisoned and killed for translating the Bible into English and many others suffered because they dared to make the text of the Bible available to the ordinary "lay" person. We still have the ridiculous concept of "lay" person and professional clergy in the church. Jesus spoke to the common people........He still does. It angered the professional religious leaders then and led to his crucifixion. It angered the religious leaders in Martin Luther's day. Anyone who spoke against the religious hierarchy of the day, "The Church" (the Roman Catholic Church) was labeled a heretic and was sentenced to death. One of the biggest offences was to say that anyone could read the Bible. And at that time the "whole world" was wrong. Don't be surprised if you discover that the status quo of "modern Christianity" doesn't match the Bible. And don't bring it up unless you want to be branded a heretic. They won't kill you today, in this country, but they will kill your testimony and make you of no effect. But then you'll understand the real "church". The real church is not big and powerful and popular and influencing government. The real church is a remnant of believers in Jesus' words. They are disciples who abide in his words and are free on the inside because they know the truth. That which is highly esteemed among men is an abomination before God. The whole world is still wrong and Jesus is right (1 Jn 2:15-17).

Faith is being sure. Faith is being certain. Belief is being sure. Belief is being certain. Hope, biblically speaking, is confidence in what is expected, not blind wishing or guessing,(1679, 1680). Faith is the surety of things we are confident are going to happen, and the proof without being able to see it. You believe that the Sun will rise in the morning. It hasn't happened yet, but you believe it will. It's not guessing or imagining or wishing. It's based on fact and experience. That 's faith, or belief; same word. "But I thought faith was not knowing what was going to happen and "hoping" it would happen anyway". That's called, "hope deferred" and it makes the heart sick! (Prov 13:12). "Desire fulfilled is a tree of life". Faith is fulfilling; it doesn't make your heart sick. There is a place for wishing upon a star and imaginations and magic with fairy dust but that's Disney not Jesus. That's Santa; not Jesus. That's flesh not Spirit. The faith of the elders caused them to be witnesses (martyrs). Only by faith can we understand that God made the worlds (billions of galaxies, each containing billions of solar systems) that can be seen from things that can't be seen. Able had confidence and certainty when he offered a blood sacrifice, because that's what he heard that God did for Adam and Eve. Cain had a "better" idea and imagined and wished and hoped that it would be just as good if not better. He was disappointed. His hope was deferred and his heart was sick. So he killed Able. Cain wanted to win and the only way he could accomplish that was to remove his opponent. Able still speaks. Enoch walked with God. And then he was not, for God took him. Now that's all we get from Genesis. But the current writer of Hebrews says that Enoch believed God and by his faith he was translated that he not see death. However, later in verse 13 he says that these ALL died. Jesus is the first resurrected from the dead (1 Cor 15:20 and knowing that in Adam ALL die :22). Enoch and Elijah did not became immortal before Jesus. They may have gone to third heaven as Paul did but they came back and died and were raised again after Jesus was raised. All the souls who had died were led out of the grave and walked the streets of Jerusalem when Jesus rose from the dead (Mt 27:52-53). Enoch was before the law was given to Moses and he was pleasing to God; not because of works but because he believed God and his works were the result of his belief. Grace produces works. Works will never produce grace. Noah found grace in the eyes of the Lord, because he believed God. "Noah, it's going to rain and I'm flooding the whole world. Build a boat for you and your family and the animals". "Rain? What's Rain? The whole world is evil"? These are questions Noah could have had but he just believed God. It seems so foreign to us that the whole world could be wrong. But it's always been that way (1 Jn 5:19 and Eph 2:2, the course of this world). "Yeah, but Glenn, in this twenty-first century, knowledge has increased and the world has gotten better and we have unity and love"! Really? All the bombings, ISIS, Aleppo, racial hatred, the elections; the world is just as hateful as its always been. I think we should look for a city having the foundations of which the builder and maker is God, like Abraham did. The world should be "foreign" to us. The things of the world should not be strangely dim, but blatantly dark. If we could time travel and you were transported to cave man days, would you fit in? The world and the things of the world should be that foreign to us. "Come on, Glenn, you have to be like the world to win the world". And that's workin' for ya'? "Yeah, look at all the churches we've got"! Okay, and you probably think we're a Christian country too, right? "Of course, we celebrate Christmas and Easter". Oy vey.

Sarah received power to conceive by faith, not because she considered herself faithful but she deemed the one having promised to be faithful. "Having faith" is not blindly hoping that we can achieve something that seems impossible. "Having faith" is believing that God will do what he said he would do. He is faithful. We trust him; that's faith. Blind faith is not faith at all. It's grasping in the dark, guessing and wishing for the best and if he that has blind faith leads another they are both blind and both will fall in the ditch.

These ALL died in faith, not having received the promises but saw them being fulfilled in the future in prophecy. They pursued the heavenly. Abel, Enoch, Noah, Abraham and Sarah all died. "But what about Enoch? He was translated that he not see death"? This comes from Genesis 5:24, "Enoch walked with God; then he was not, for God took him". This doesn't necessarily mean that Enoch stayed in heaven. He may have only visited as Paul did. Jesus is the first resurrected man to receive an immortal body. Elijah went up in a chariot but came back and wrote a letter to Jehoram, (2 Chron 21:12). Then Elijah died. These ALL died. Enoch died. Lazarus was raised but not to immortality. Lazarus died again and awaits the second coming of Christ when those who are asleep in Christ will rise first. Christ is the Firstfruits, the first raised from the dead to immortality (1 Cor 15: 20-23). Christ's sacrifice paved the way to be resurrected. No one could enter heaven until Adam's sin had been punished and the sentence had been paid in full. Enoch and Elijah were both members of Adam's fallen race and needed redemption. They had to wait for the Messiah. "Where's Lazarus now"? You mean his body? "Yes". It's in the ground. "Okay, his soul then"? It's sleeping, like a coma. "But our denomination doesn't believe in "soul sleep". Well, maybe they don't know everything. "Those who are asleep in Christ will rise first"(1 Thes 4:13-18). When Lazarus died, Jesus said he was sleeping. And Mark 5:39, "The child is........ sleeping". Of course these are only my deductions from what Jesus said. I don't know the future; no one does. But I'm not worried because Jesus is faithful and therefore I have faith.

When Abraham offered up Isaac, his only begotten, because in Isaac would Abraham's seed be called, this was a type of the messiah that was to come. Abraham believed that God could raise Isaac from the dead. Evidently, Abraham needed this experience so that <u>he</u> would know that in all things he could trust God. God tested him for his own confidence. God was not trying to find out if Abraham would hold back. God knows everything. Sometimes God tests us so it builds our confidence. Struggles make us stronger. "What if we fail the test"? You can have a do-over. "I think I've had a lot of do-overs". Haven't we all?

Then there's Jacob and Esau, which was supposed to be Esau and Jacob. Esau was the eldest of the twins but he gave up his birthright to his younger twin. But God knew this would happen. God had even said that he loved Jacob and hated Esau when the twins were still in the womb! God knew. Esau was a profane person (12:16). Some think that God made Esau profane. I don't think that God made Esau so that God could watch him burn eternally and find some kind of joy in watching the flames melt the flesh off of Esau eternally and listen to his eternal screams. That sounds more like a zombie movie than the merciful Creator. "So what then"? I think that we are all born into the world spiritually dead. We are no more spiritually aware of God than other mammals. We have a developed intellect but not spirit. When we become born of the Spirit we become spiritually alive, born, born of the Spirit; alive to God and dead to sin. We become spirit-beings. We own a mind and we own a body but we are children of God. I don't think mammals, no matter how developed their minds are go to hell and burn for eternity. I think the Devil and his angels do. I think those who do not become born from above meet the same destiny as other mammals; the grave, Hades; Gehenna, the valley of Hinnon, death; they cease to exist. "But what about justice? What about me getting to see people that have wronged me going to hell and burning forever"? I think we should stop thinking like that. You don't know of what spirit you are (Lk 9:55). Do you really want justice? For you? Oh, just for them. Jesus paid for the justice you deserved and he also paid for every whole person, every child of God, spirit, soul and body (1 Thes 5:23).

As I research words and ideas from the original language and some of the other theories out there, I realize that whatever is published and read is subject to criticism. I realize that when I say, "I think" that the information I am giving is only theory, however it's what I believe with the information I have. If I happen to ever sell significant volumes of my books, I know there will be critics, skeptics and those who will want to discredit me to discredit the information in my books. It always happens. There are standard arguments to Calvinism and Arminianism that can go on ad infinitum. There's Catholic and protestant, and all kinds of conspiracy theories with all kinds of pros and cons. I simply desire that the reader, you, read the Bible for yourself, ask God to speak to your heart through his words and believe him. Just know that just because someone seems to discredit another, it doesn't prove that either is right or wrong. Discrediting the witness is an old tactic when one doesn't have sufficient content to refute the information that the witness is giving. I've had this done to me many times. It just proves to me that the opposition doesn't have enough evidence to back up his argument. I'm not trying to take on the religious leaders of our day. Jesus did and it got him crucified. The same happens when someone tries to take on the medical leaders or the political parties that run this country. All the dirt comes out and some of the dirt is manufactured or distorted through the largest news media conglomerates with the most money. An old saying, "Don't throw the baby out with the bath water". Yeah, that's pretty old and would have to be explained to some. The point is, if something is true, let's keep that and build on it. Satan quoted scripture to Jesus. The scripture is true. Satan is the ultimate proven false witness but that doesn't mean that what he quoted is false. I say all this to preserve some of the ideas I write about no matter what is said or distorted about me. And that will only happen if any of my books become even mildly popular at all. I'm also saying this about other writers who have taken on the establishment and have been "discredited", especially in the field of alternative medicine. Truth is truth and we should embrace it; it makes us free. Drinking plenty of water and eating your fruits and veggies will probably make you healthier and you've heard this from plenty of sources. However, it won't make anybody any money and requires discipline. So the vast majority of Americans, especially children won't do it. Drugs are easy to take and make lots of money. Just sayin'. Beware of the easy way out and follow the money. On the other hand, there are reasons to go to the doctor. The responsibility is on our shoulders to choose how to solve life's problems. Thinking is becoming a lost art. We should study. We should learn. We should take responsibility for our own choices. "Okay, okay, I get it, but right now you're making my head hurt, I need a candy bar and entertainment". Gotcha. But when you come back we'll talk more. Remember there is no condemnation. So have a glass of wine or a beer and watch a movie or eat some chocolate. But don't get drunk and have a better menu than a steady diet of junk food. "Glenn! I can't believe you said to consume alcohol. Don't you know it's of the Devil"? The leaders of your denomination in Europe drink beer together (not get drunk) and it's not a sin over there. I can see it now, "Glenn's advice for feeling condemned is to drink alcohol and eat chocolate". Nice. Well, you get the picture.

Meanwhile back at the kingdom of God, Hebrews chapter eleven, Jacob and Esau. By faith Isaac blessed Jacob and Esau. "But Jacob swindled Esau out of his birthright". Actually, Esau counted his birthright as worthless because he was hungry. Hmmmmmmm. Bodily appetites? Or spiritual blessings? Esau made his own choices. "But God knew before they were born that this would happen". He did. "So did Esau go to hell"? Here we go again, we seem to be preoccupied with the idea that people go to hell and the reason to "accept" Christ is to avoid hell. "Well, that's what's preached. Ever heard of "Sinners in the hands of an angry God"? It's like really famous". Yeah, about that, I think that hell was made for the Devil and his angels. I don't think anyone else goes there. "How can you say that and call yourself a Christian"? God is more merciful than we think. The older I get the more merciful I see him. We need to ask ourselves what that tendency is, to think "other" people are going to get what they deserve, Hell. It's not mercy. It's not justice, because we're no better. "Well, but I chose Christ"! Oh, I thought he chose you. I think we should not judge. And that's a period.

By faith, Jacob blessed the sons of Joseph. Ephraim and Manasseh. "But Jacob (Israel) blessed them backwards by crossing his arms"! (Gen 48:14ff) Maybe God knows things we don't and we're the ones who are backwards. Moses counted the reproach of Christ greater riches than the treasures of Egypt. Christ? Yes. The prophets, including Moses looked for and desired the Messiah! (the Christ) (1 Pet 1:10-12). Okay, so this is also going to sound odd. There are parts of the Hebrew Bible (the Tanakh) what we call the "old testament" that are new testament. The Messianic Psalms are new testament; the prophecies in Isaiah concerning the Messiah are new testament because they are about the Messiah, the Christ. Any prophecy by any "old testament" prophet about the Messiah is new testament. And there are parts of what we call the new testament that are old testament. Taking the offering for healing to the priest is old testament even though Jesus said to do it. One of the hardest concepts to swallow is that most, like ninety five percent, of Jesus' teachings are in the old testament to people who were under the law, the old testament. He taught them how to keep the law with new testament principles. Not an eye for an eye but turn the other cheek. Jesus was also teaching them how to survive in an oppressed society. We in twenty first century America are not in an oppressed society (well, not legally; there are many neighborhoods where minorities live in oppression) so we wouldn't need to learn how to survive in an oppressed society. We can't apply turn the other cheek. "But it's red words". I know. And because of the death and resurrection of Jesus we are forgiven of ALL our sins, even though Jesus said, "If you do not forgive men their sins neither will your Father forgive your sins" (Mt 6:14). Yes, they are red words but we also need context. To whom was he speaking? And when was he speaking? (in the context of old or new covenant?). Also, there are passages where Jesus is speaking and it seems to end and then gospel writer is speaking but it continues in red. One place that seems to happen is John chapter three. Jesus is speaking and there is a natural end to his thought at the end of verse fifteen. However it is commonly continued in red, implying that Jesus said everything right up to the end of verse twenty one. I believe these words are true but I'm not convinced Jesus said them. The only reason I bring this up is because the words of Jesus are God's words and they are usually referred to as red words. But just because they may be red in your Bible doesn't mean that they are Christ's words. When it says, "Jesus said", then its Jesus' words and like we said earlier, the context can make all the difference in understanding what he's saying and what he's not saying. The apostles might have felt like, "Why did you say that, Jesus? You were doing so good and now this", for example John 6:53; "Unless you eat the flesh of the Son of man……..". After that he had to ask them, "Will you go away also"? I believe we grow in spirit when we seek understanding instead of skipping verses that Jesus spoke with an excuse like, "It's just too hard to understand". Most preachers don't use the words of Jesus. They prefer Paul and that's why if you say Jesus' words are the word of God and Paul's words are Paul's words they get infuriated because they want to say that they are preaching the word of God but at the same time put Jesus' words on a shelf. There are the words of God and there are the words that agree with the words of God and I value them equally. But there are words in the Bible that do not agree with Jesus' words and they are just not the word of God. "But they are in the Bible"! Exactly. "You're saying the Bible is wrong"? No. I'm saying the Bible (which only means book) is a collection of words and thoughts from many different people and cultures and even the Devil is quoted. The Bible is true. The Bible has no errors. However, some of the writers and speakers did. The Devil is quoted and he is a liar. "There are lies in the Bible"? Yes. "Heretic! Blasphemer!" Stop. The Bible is true and inerrant in that it records words correctly in the original language. However, when Peter told Jesus not to go to the cross, that was Satan speaking and Jesus told him so (Mt 16:23). "But it's in the Bible"! Exactly.

By faith Moses left Egypt, not fearing the king, and kept on as seeing the invisible one. No one has seen God who is the invisible One. But Moses kept on as if he did, because he heard him. Hear him. And he speaks through his Son in these last days. Hear the words of Jesus. Jesus is God and his words are God's words. "You're repeating yourself". Now were getting somewhere. Jesus is our Passover. They passed through the Red Sea, as a type of baptism (1 Cor 10:2, spiritual food, spiritual drink, spiritual rock, Christ); notice they were dry, a type of baptism in spirit not water. By faith Rahab the harlot...... "What? How can a harlot have faith? John 9:31 says that God doesn't hear the prayers of sinners"! Actually the blind man said that, not the Bible. "But it's in the Bible"! Which can only mean that God didn't say everything that is in the Bible. In other words the Bible is not the word of God. "The tax collectors and harlots go before you into the kingdom of God" (Mt 21:31), Jesus, speaking to the chief priests and elders. And the only thing some will get out of this whole chapter even this whole book will be that, "Glenn said, "the Bible is not the word of God". And Jesus said he would tear down the Temple and rebuild it again in three days. There will always be plenty of those around who would take words and meanings out of context. As I write this Donald and Hillary are battling to be elected. Do you think anything that any one has said has been distorted by the news? There are more examples of faith than time allows us to mention, we just need to read our Bibles, cover to cover. "I thought you didn't believe the Bible"? Is that what you thought? But there were also those who didn't seem to "win" by faith. Their faith led them to death. They received mockings of trials, floggings, prison, and they were stoned. They were sawn in two. They died by the sword. They were in need, afflicted, ill-treated, wandering in deserts, and mountains and caves. This they all did by faith. Faith isn't worldly success. Faith doesn't bring worldly or physical success. Faith more often brings suffering and forgiveness in this world and glory in the next. We can live in the Spirit now; we can live in eternal life now by enduring undeserved suffering and forgiveness. "Is there another way"? No. "If anyone desires to come after me, let him deny himself, and let him bear his cross, and let him follow me" (Mt 16:24). "But I thought……..". Blessed are the poor in spirit, they that mourn, they that hunger for justice, the persecuted, the merciful, the meek, the pure. "That's blessing"? Blessings are spiritual; they are now but they are spiritual in the heavenly realm. "What about prospering"? You mean money? You can't serve God and money. You will love the one and hate the other. "That's a hard saying". Look at verse forty, "God having foreseen something better concerning us……..". Remember, he is more merciful than we think. Take heart we're ready for chapter twelve.

12

The Church

There is discipline which makes disciplined ones or disciples and there is punishment. Jesus has taken all our punishment. He does, however, let us suffer the consequences of our own choices. Discipline teaches us what to do in the future. Punishment is payment for what we've done in the past. Jesus paid for all the punishment due us, past, present and future. He paid at the cross and he paid in the grave and rose again. It is finished. We continue to be discipled, or learn obedience through the things we suffer just as Jesus did. He chastises us by letting us reap the results of our own poor judgment. This is good parenting. We learn. We learn to spend wisely. We learn to take care of the temple we occupy, our bodies. We learn to be generous. We learn to treat others the way we want to be treated. We learn to love the way Jesus loves. It may take a lifetime but we learn that relationships are the most valuable commodities we have. We have tons of examples who have gone on before us and if we keep them in mind, those just mentioned in chapter eleven, we find the confidence and desire to lay aside every temptation. Speed is not needed to run a long race, patience is. It's a long race. We can only endure if joy is set before us. Learning to enjoy the journey is a challenge. But knowing that the journey is constantly preparing us for the destination helps. It's a long race. Young people say, "Life is short". Old people know better. It's long and hard. I can't imagine life without Jesus. I don't know how married people stay married without

Jesus. Without Jesus we are dust in the wind or as James puts it "a vapor". All the money in the world can't buy time and can't guarantee health. And when this body dies, then what? That's the big question. For those of us born of the Spirit, we live eternally. For those that aren't ? Well, we don't know. Oh we think we know. But we don't know. One thing is for sure, they don't live eternally. There is a resurrection of judgment. Not for those who have been paid for. There is, "Depart from me, I never knew you". There is the grave, death, Hades, Sheol, Gehenna and there is one mention of Tartarus, all these words translated as "hell". Tartarus is reserved for the Devil and his angels (2 Pet 2:4). The rest of these words simply mean the grave, the end of life, ceasing to exist. "But Jesus said, "Fire". True, but the garbage dump outside the city of Jerusalem that he referred to, The Valley of Hinnom or Gehenna continually smoldered, burning the trash. I don't believe any animal, any mammal, any beast is going to Tartarus (what we imagine hell to be), but that they perish, cease to exist, as did the trash at the garbage dump. I also believe that any "human" is a just mammal until "born" from above, just dust in the wind, a vapor; all flesh is as grass. Made from dust, to dust it returns but the spirit lives forever and gets a new mind and a new body (Gen 3:19 and Jn 11:25-26). And if that mammal doesn't receive the Spirit, the born from above experience, it remains just a mammal, however intelligent it may be, still just a mammal and mammals don't go to Tartarus or the place that has been described like "Dante's Inferno". "Glenn, how can you be so sure"? This is what I'm sure about right now. Like we said before, no one knows the future and our theology is always changing, hopefully coming closer and closer to the truth.

One thing that is constant in my journey is that God is becoming more and more merciful in my eyes. He is the Redeemer. He is the Savior. That's his nature and that's what he does; he saves. The name Jesus means "Yahweh Saves". We sing "There's power in the name of Jesus". We sing "There's something about that name". And there is. If we can use for a fact that, name means character, then we start knowing God as Savior. Everything else is based on that. In the beginning man had a choice ; he chose wrongly and since then God has been saving mankind. First he covered man's sins with sacrifices. Then he donned a fleshly body and sacrificed that body for the cleansing and forgiving of all man's sin. He came in the "likeness" of sinful flesh to redeem us, to save us; not to give us another choice. Our Calvinist friends got this half right. There is nothing in lost mankind that can choose good. We are born into this world the slaves of sin. God chooses us. God puts his Spirit into us then we can choose good. "But why did Jesus say, "Repent for the kingdom of heaven has drawn near"? He was speaking to those under the law, in the old covenant. The word repent is translated from "metanoia" and means to change your thinking, which they could do. Jesus would go on to say that you cannot see the kingdom of heaven unless you are "born" of the Spirit (Jn 3). This is how he would build his congregation, the church, "ekklesia", and the gates of Hades (the grave, death) would not prevail against it. He had said, "The Holy Spirit is with you, but he will be IN you"! The Church would be an inside thing. The Church would be internal and the fruit would be external. The Church would be the New Testament in his death (shed blood) and resurrection, the Church of the only begotten and the firstborn ones. Jesus is the head of the Church and his born from above followers are the body. No buildings, no politics, no externals except the fruit of the Spirit which is Love. The Church started out as Jewish believers loving one another and then included all nations. Sadly, as the Church grew it was infiltrated by wolves and turned into a political, social and financial conglomerate headed by Rome. It wasn't the church anymore. It was the Roman Catholic Church. Since then every denomination and even those who are called "non-denominational" has had its beginning in the political and financial entity called the Roman Catholic Church. The Church was struggling but was still The Church until it became Roman. Then it became political and although the whole system influences the whole world today, it's not The Church. No wonder other religions hate it. It's become obsessed with relics and money and concerned with the politics of nations. We were never meant to be in politics. That's what corrupted the church in the first place. Well, the real Church had to go underground. The real Church is still alive and is scattered everywhere. Real saints are in organizations called churches everywhere but we are scattered and not in unity. "Glenn, I go to church every Sun Day, pay my tithes, have been baptized in water, take communion, celebrate Christmas and Easter and listen to Christian radio. I go to Christian concerts and conferences. I read all the latest books on Christian living and Christian fiction. Doesn't that make me a true Christian, part of the Church"? NO. "What if I read your books? Will that make me a Christian"? NO. "What then"? You must be born from above. Your life, your fruit must show change of nature. Old nature (dead to God and alive to sin) must die to sin and a divine new nature must replace it and become alive to God. You must become a new creature in Christ. "How"? Ask. "What if I'm just scared of going to hell and ask God to rescue me"? Well, it was never intended that way but God rescues; that's what he does. The "Christian religion" is based on fear but that's not how it started. Perfect love casts out fear but in the political, financial, social institution called "church" fear casts out love. If you're tired of performing for approval in church then come to Jesus. "I will give you rest.......rest for your soul, my yoke is easy and my burden is light" (Mt 11: 28-30).

If you read books like, *The Two Babylons* by Alexander Hislop and *Babylon Mystery Religion* by Ralph Woodrow, you'll find a lot of history where the gates of Hades did prevail against the Roman Catholic Church showing that it is not the true Church. There have been people like Francis of Assisi (his real name, Giovanni di Pietro di Bernardone), Martin Luther, Mother Teresa and Henry Nouwen who were all Roman Catholic but obviously followers of Christ. These are a few examples of the true Church scattered in the organized political, social and financial institution called church. There are remnants of the true Church in every denomination and country in the world. The gates of Hades haven't prevailed against the true Church. The protestant churches are no exception, with all the scandals both sexual and financial. They just were not the true church no matter how big or popular they were. "But I got saved by watching one of these "fallen" ministers on television". God can use a donkey; "The dumb ass speaking with a man's voice" (2 Pet 2:16). The Church has not fallen. The Church is working. The Church is not full of hypocrites and scam artists and liars and fake "healers". That's the circus. And there are many three ring circuses performing every Sun Day morning and especially on E-Astar Sun rise morning, followed by chocolate bunnies laying painted eggs and hatching marshmallow chicks. If you want to confuse a child, just sayin'. Then there's Xmas, yes, please leave the Christ out of Roman Catholic "Christ's Mass", he's got nothing to do with it. If we stop lying to our kids about Christmas and Easter they might have a chance at believing when we talk about Jesus. "Glenn, that sounds harsh"! What the organized "church" has done in the name of Christianity is harsh. Ask a Muslim whose ancestors' heads rolled by the Crusaders because they refused to be baptized in water and follow the corrupt "church of Rome". That's harsh. The Spanish Inquisition was harsh. Burning martyrs at the stake was harsh. Just because it's sugar-coated (or chocolate coated) now doesn't make it any less harsh.

Let's not confuse punishment and discipline. Discipline teaches us about the future, to not make the same mistake twice. Punishment is revenge, payback, getting even. Father disciplines us by allowing us to suffer from our own mistakes. I've heard some say, "God slapped me upside the head with a two by four to get my attention" (add southern drawl for emphasis). That's not God. That might be your earthly dad or redneck culture but it's not God. He has a still small voice. He doesn't yell. He doesn't need to. The biggest clue to a child is when his parent yells; then he knows the parent has lost control. God whispers. We should listen. Be still, then you can know that he is God. "You sound so sure". These are Bible verses I just didn't look them up for you. So when you are disciplined, straighten up and strengthen your knees and be healed. Pursue peace and holiness. Choose grace. Avoid bitterness and unforgiveness lest you fall like Esau. We are not in the old covenant, the mountain that burned with fire and doom and gloom, that of which even Moses was terrified. But we have come near to a heavenly Jerusalem, and to angels too many to count. And to a gathering of the Church of firstborn ones recorded in heaven; to Jesus, the mediator, of the NEW Covenant. The kingdom of heaven is unshakeable therefore let us have grace. God is the judge of all. God is a consuming fire. Let's not pretend to know who or how he judges. We should be giving grace not calling down fire from heaven. "But what about Jesus saying to heap coals of fire on their heads"? What? You're not listening. That was an old custom. They carried coals of fire in clay containers on pads of cloth on their heads to bring to a neighbor to start a fire when the neighbor's fire had gone out, so they could be warm and cook. "Oh". Can we stop trying to burn people? Love one another as I have loved you! Love one another!

13

Conclusion

It still seems to me that different contributors added to this letter in its early stages as it circulated, especially this chapter. It seems to be full of "random" exhortations for general use within the Church. Let brotherly love continue. That should be our default setting. Instead of criticizing other churches we should be loving them. Christianity was meant to be loving, kind and inclusive. Some of the attitudes I've seen have been critical, divisive, exclusive and downright mean-spirited. Not all would admit it but the attitude of some churches is "If you don't do things the way we do it, y'all are going to hell". Well, there it is again, the religion built on fear not love. We have to "let" brotherly love continue. It's deliberate. We go out of our way to help someone else connect and stay connected. We all need that at some point. I was asked to leave church staff after being there for eighteen years because my theology was different. I get that. But since I've left not one person has called to see how I'm doing. We were supposed to be family. We were supposed to have brotherly love. It's too bad and it's not an isolated story. This happens to many people all the time. It hurts. Churches hurt people because it's a social organization and if you're not in the "click", you're out. Money keeps you in some churches, but usually it's compliance. Don't rock the boat. Just keep doing what everybody else does and don't have a difference of opinion. Most of all always agree with the "Pastor's" "vision". It's sad but love has nothing to do with being in the political, social and financial organization called "church". "Glenn, you're just saying that because you got your feelings hurt". There were many. But it is true that you see more clearly when it happens to you. I can give you at least ten other staffers who got the boot and then that's it, you just don't see them anymore. I suppose we have to "have" love before we can let love continue. I wonder why the writer thought the readers had to be told to love people. Why did they have to be reminded to be hospitable? They were reminded to visit the imprisoned, and these weren't criminals; these were those in chains because they followed Jesus. And the readers had to be reminded to visit them! And be mindful of the ill-treated, since you are in the body yourself. In other words it could happen to you too. If you go to a church, it's great to socialize with others in the church, but it would be kind to reach out to any who don't go anymore. Wonder why they don't go anymore? "Oh, we know why they don't go to church; and we don't want to get dragged down with them". Nice. "Love one another as I have loved you".

Then he seems to be saying adultery and fornication are wrong and God will judge you, so if you want to be sexually active get married. That was an issue then and it is an issue now. Adultery and fornication hurt the people doing it. The consequences are bad enough without throwing, "God's gonna git you" in there. The writer wants us to love and be kind but also have a judgmental attitude. That's a contradiction. "But it's in the Bible". We've been through this. Don't judge. Just don't. We can't. "But he says God will judge". Yes, he does, from the lofty position of "I know God's going to judge you because you're sinning. Your sin is a different sin than mine but I know that he's going to judge you". He continues with admonishing about loving money. Church people do that? I think there's a whole doctrine of "prosperity" that is money-loving and has no contentment with being satisfied with what we have. The Lord is my help and I shouldn't be afraid, but I must confess I still fret about what man does to me; I have a long way to go on this one. It's rejection and I know that they are wrong for rejecting me but still...........

He says remember your leaders. I would say watch your leaders. If they are servants then follow but if they are concerned with popularity then choose to be a servant anyway and don't follow the temptation to compete for popularity. A jealous leader is easily intimidated. Consider the issue of their conduct and imitate their faith not their flaws. Jesus is always first. Jesus is the same. Jesus' words always take precedence. If anyone teaches against that, don't be carried away with strange teaching. Now, granted if the status quo today is that Paul's writings are just as much God's word as Jesus' words and you say different, you will be thought strange. But here it is clear that the writer is putting Jesus first. Paul may and does change. Peter, James, John; they all change. Jesus doesn't change. His words are God's words and they are timeless.

Back to verse 2. Some have entertained angels and were not aware of it. Apparently, when this was written angels were visiting people and no one could tell the difference between an angel and a person. So how did they know they were angels? Maybe after the visit they realized that this person didn't really exist. In chapter eleven we learned that we have come to an innumerable company of angels. Is it possible that there are innumerable angels among us now? What about angels of darkness that transform themselves into angels of light? Are there more of them than us? What about natural brute beasts as Peter and Jude call them, that look like people? What if there are few that are real humans born of the Spirit and the rest, the many are in one of these other categories. What we do know is that few will enter in at the narrow gate that leads to life and many will go into the broad gate that leads to death (not Tartarus). What we do know is that there were creatures, angels, walking around in the first century that looked like ordinary people. And why would they be here? To test us? To help us? I'm not sure, but they are here and we are exhorted to be hospitable because we may be entertaining them. This isn't Halloween; this is real and is really going on among us. It may be easier to believe that a stranger that you see once and then they vanish was an angel, but what if you've known them your whole life and you watched them grow and have a family and have a job and appear to be just a regular person? "No, God wouldn't do that". Why not? "That's too much; that's stretching it a bit". Did you know that terrorists do this? Do you know that there are thousands of sleepers among us that are just waiting for a chance to destroy this country? Did you know they have families and go to church and take flying lessons and are in government positions and go undetected? "Oh, Glenn, that's just a conspiracy theory". Tell that to the survivors of 911. "Okay, but those were real people". I think terrorists are without a conscience which makes them no more human than animals at best and possibly demons. Sounds spooky? Have you noticed man's fascination with the dark side of the supernatural? Vampires, Zombies, the walking dead, shape shifting and animorphing are all very popular now, not to mention that Halloween has been dragged out to last a whole month. Of course that's Hollywood but for every counterfeit there is something real. I don't think the thirteenth chapter Hebrews was meant to be scary, but just know that there are principalities and powers and rulers of darkness and angels and creatures among us. The Lord is our help; we will not be afraid of man or them. If we focus on the spirit realm we will always be aware of HIS presence, "I will never leave you, nor will I ever forsake you". "For I am persuaded that neither death, nor life, nor angels, nor rulers, nor powers, nor things present, nor things to come, nor height, nor depth, nor any other creature will be able to separate us from the love of God in Christ Jesus our Lord" (Rom 8:38). "…..a thorn in the flesh was given to me, a messenger (angel in Greek) of Satan, that he might buffet me" (2 Cor 12: 7). "We are not wrestling against flesh and blood, but against the rulers, against the authorities, against the rulers of this world, of the darkness of this age, against the spiritual powers of evil in the heavenlies" (Eph 6:12). We just need to be aware that we do not war against the flesh and much of our fight has to do with our own imaginations and thoughts against the knowledge of God (2 Cor 10:3-6). There are other beings walking among us, but our fight as "born ones" is not with them. Our fight is in the mind. We need to arm ourselves with God's thoughts. We need to think like Jesus. And there is no other way to train our minds to think like Jesus than to meditate on HIS words. The words he speaks are spirit and life. "I am with you all the days until the completion of the age" (Mt 28:20). "I will not leave you orphans; I am coming to you" (Jn 14:18). "And I give them eternal life, and they shall never perish, neither shall anyone snatch them out of my hand" (Jn 10: 28).

Apparently there was division in the body of Christ about those who eat only herbs and veggies and those who eat everything, meat. Of course even today eating meat is questionable for vegetarians and especially those who make a religion out of it. I've been a vegetarian before and it seems to be a healthy way to live. However, I know Jesus ate fish and ate lamb at least once a year. In Romans fourteen Paul tells the church to quit judging each other by what you eat. The point was to quit judging each other. Here in twenty-first century America, we don't eat cat or dog or horse meat. In first century Israel or Palestine they just didn't eat pig or shellfish or camel or any of the "forbidden" meats described as unclean in Leviticus chapter eleven. It was not only Jewish but also Palestinian. Here in Hebrews 13: 9 the writer isn't referring to clean or unclean because that was already the custom for Hebrews, much the same as our culture is not eating cats and dogs. We wouldn't have to say to anyone, "Don't judge me for eating cats and mice, because none of us do. The "strange teaching" here would be the same as in Romans fourteen. Some thought they were more spiritual because they only ate vegetables and judged others for eating (clean) meats. Then there is the reference to the animals (meat) offered in the tabernacle. The clean animals' blood was spilled and offered and the meat was not to be eaten but was burned outside the camp. In like manner, Jesus' body suffered outside the gate. This was shameful, a reproach, a curse, like a common thief. Our reward, esteem, self-worth doesn't come from this world which is "inside the gate" (that which is highly esteemed among men); our reward is in heaven, in the spirit realm, which is why we seek the city that is coming. This is not our home. We're just passing through. Don't get too comfortable. Worried about the presidential election? Stock market? That's not our realm. This is not our home. Don't store up earthly moth ridden and rusted treasures. "Well, should we vote"? Why? Especially this year, why? "Well, you know, the lesser of two evils". Don't get entangled in another man's warfare. Store up treasures in heaven. And heaven is where not when. Heaven is the spirit realm where our spirit, the real us, lives. When our bodies die we don't go to heaven; our bodies change and they go to heaven. Our spirit is already in the heavenlies, the spirit realm. Why are we so concerned and consumed by the plastic, temporary cosmos run by evil. You want the lesser of two evils; or the good? We should go outside the camp and bear his reproach. We should avoid that which is highly exalted among men. It's an abomination to God. "What about our favorite movie stars and singers and rappers"? I listen to all kinds of music but none are my idol. Whomever you spend more time with is your idol. Spending time with Jesus is reading and meditating on HIS words, red ones. This is how we learn to think like Jesus. Some people think in Bible verses. That's a good start, but we need to think biblically not think only

Bible verses. We can think scripturally or think in scriptures. We can think red verses or we can think like Jesus. The idea is to be able to hear Jesus speak and apply his character to our twenty-first century situations. What would Jesus think? And then we will know what he would do. The first step is to become detached to things and people. "What about family? Family is everything". If we detach from family and then connect with family with Jesus principles we have a real connection. Flesh and blood will never give us a real connection. "Blood's thicker than water"! What the heck does that mean? "My family is everything and I'm not gonna let religion or politics get in the way". Jesus said, "Who is my mother, my brothers........but they that hear the will of God and do it"(Mt 12:47, 10:34ff). Our real family are the ones who are Christ followers. The flesh family, unless they are Christ followers, are those who need to hear Jesus words, potential faith family. We don't know who is predestined to be a Christ follower but neither do we know who isn't. We can know them by their fruit, but I don't know for sure, nor do I know someone who does. We should share the good news with everyone. Because we don't know like God knows. Everyone is a potential child of God to us because we don't know the future. However, if we think someone died without "finding God" we can know that they were just a form, a body, and that body died and dust returned to dust and no one is burning in hell. "What about the rich man and Lazarus"? Yeah, I know. We talked about that in chapter five. I still don't know the full meaning of that parable. But it is a parable, for he didn't speak to the crowds or Pharisees (Lk 16:15) without one. And parables were used to hide the meaning not clear it up (Mt 13:10-17 and 34-35). "You mean we won't see them again"? I'm not sure what bodies look like in heaven but it will be our spirit connection that we will recognize. If all we had was a flesh connection, we won't have it anymore. "Well, that makes sense, but......never mind. That does make sense". Someone once said that "it's not what we don't know that hurts us, it's when we don't know that we don't know". Some things we just don't know and it's good to know that we don't know. God is the judge. He'll sort it all out and we are going to like it. "Well, if God's got it all figured out and knows who's going where and what's what, why should we even preach the gospel"? Because he may want to use you. Do you want to be used by God? "Well, if I don't share the good news, he'll just use someone else". Yes, but don't you want to be used? We're just not responsible for others' outcomes and no one is going to hell except fallen angels.

"Then through him let us offer up a sacrifice of praise to God always, that is, the fruit of the lips, confessing to his name. But do not be forgetful of doing good and sharing, for God is well pleased with such sacrifices". The writer in verses 15-16 is encouraging us to share the gospel and share our stuff but mostly confessing his name, his character, the fruit of our lips. This last part verses 18-24 seem to be a general closing to be circulated with this letter. Peitho, (3982) means to trust or have confidence in your leaders more than to obey. It means to be persuaded. It means they have earned your trust or confidence not blind obedience. Pray for them because that changes our attitude and we are able to yield and conduct ourselves well. Most bibles use the words "obey, submit and behave. The real meanings of these words are trust, yield and conduct yourself, in which we control ourselves not have someone control us. Why are bibles translated in a way to control people? It's not God's idea. Now that we've got that straight, we can receive the God of peace. He can perfect us through the great shepherd, the one who was raised from the dead in the new covenant, Jesus Christ. He will be perfecting us, in every good work, doing his will. Jesus gets the glory, not our valiant efforts. And it seems that Paul at least wrote this last little addition about Timothy and being freed and those from Italy greet you. Amen.

Writing this book has caused me to rethink what I believe and I've had to go back and rewrite a lot of the manuscript in the earlier chapters. I look forward to more change, in the right direction, for change is growth. I encourage you to let Jesus' words change your thinking also.

Printed in the United States
By Bookmasters